American Government
Using MicroCase® ExplorIt
Seventh Edition

Michael Corbett
Ball State University

Barbara Norrander
University of Arizona

WADSWORTH
™
THOMSON LEARNING

Australia • Canada • Mexico • Singapore • Spain • United Kingdom • United States

Political Science Editor: Clark Baxter
Senior Development Editor: Sharon Adams Poore
Editorial Assistant: Jonathan Katz
Assistant Editor: Julie Iannacchino
Marketing Manager: Diane McOscar

MicroCase Consultant: Julie Aguilar
Software, Lead Developer: David Simmons
Data Archivists: Meredith Reitman, Chris Bader, Matt Bahr
Production: Jodi Gleason
Copy Editor: Margaret Moore

Printed in Canada
    2   3   4   5   6   7   05   04   03   02

ISBN 0-534-58635-X

For more information, contact
Wadsworth/Thomson Learning
10 Davis Drive
Belmont, CA 94002-3098
USA

For more information about our products, contact us:
Thomson Learning Academic Resource Center
1-800-423-0563
http://www.wadsworth.com

International Headquarters
Thomson Learning
International Division
290 Harbor Drive, 2nd Floor
Stamford, CT 06902-7477
USA

UK/Europe/Middle East/South Africa
Thomson Learning
Berkshire House
168-173 High Holborn
London WC1V 7AA
United Kingdom

Asia
Thomson Learning
60 Albert Complex, #15-01
Singapore 189969

Canada
Nelson Thomson Learning
1120 Birchmount Road
Toronto, Ontario M1K 5G4
Canada

CONTENTS

Acknowledgments

Preface

Getting Started

ACKNOWLEDGMENTS

We have assumed co-authorship of this book starting with the seventh edition. Given that there have already been six successful previous editions, we take on this co-authorship with great humility and we readily acknowledge that we are standing on the shoulders of the many contributors who have gone before us. This book has had many "authors" who have helped to shape the topics and assignments. Further, we acknowledge the contributions of instructors who were willing to try something new. Because so many people who teach American government really care, we can continue to improve our computer-based approach to "hands-on" learning.

We wish to thank Sharon Adams Poore at Wadsworth Publishing for her editorial overview, and we received valuable assistance from Julie Aguilar, MicroCase Consultant at Wadsworth Publishing Company.

We would like to acknowledge the contribution of Rodney Stark at the University of Washington, who first developed the format used in this series of introductory workbooks. His leadership in making real data analysis accessible to students has transformed the way many teach introductory social science courses. Special thanks goes to Meredith Reitman, who oversaw much of the development, organization, and cleaning of the data files for this project.

We would like to thank a number of individuals and institutions who provided us with the data files upon which most of these exercises are based. The inclusion of selected variables from the American National Election Study would not have been possible without the generous help and permission of Steven Rosenstone and the National Election Studies, Institute for Social Research at the University of Michigan. We also thank the Inter-university Consortium for Political and Social Research for their permission to use the NES data. Special thanks goes to Tom W. Smith at the National Opinion Research Center for his continued direction and administration of the General Social Survey. Many of the international variables are based on the World Values Survey, for which we must thank Ronald Inglehart at The Institute for Social Research, University of Michigan. Professor Inglehart's book *Modernization and Postmodernization: Cultural, Economic and Political Change in 43 Societies* (Princeton, 1997) provided the inspiration for a number of examples in this workbook. The Center for the American Woman and Politics at the Eagleton Institute of Politics at Rutgers University also provided very useful data.

Finally, we would like to thank the following individuals who have contributed to this edition or previous editions: Gary Aguiar, Texas A & M International University; John B. Ashby, Northern Michigan University; Lindsey Back, Morehead State University; Martha Bailey, Southern Illinois University at Edwardsville; Hal Barger, Trinity University; Devin Bent, James Madison University; John Berg, Suffolk University; Milton Boykin, The Citadel; Robert Bradley, Illinois State University;

Chalmers Brumbaugh, Elon College; Jeri Cabot, College of Charleston; Sara B. Crook, Peru State College; Roy Dawes, Gettysburg College; Robert J. Duffy, Rider College; Leonard Faulk, SUNY at Fredonia; William Flanigan, University of Minnesota; Richard Fulton, Northwest Missouri State University; Tucker Gibson, Trinity University; John Hibbing, University of Nebraska–Lincoln; Laurence F. Jones, Angelo State University; Nancy Kindred, McNeil High School; Karen King, Bowling Green State University; Nancy Kral, North Harris Montgomery College District; Peter Maier, University of Wisconsin–Milwaukee; Theresa Marchant-Shapiro, Union College; Suzanne M. Marilley, Capital University; David McLaughlin, Northwest Missouri State University; Scott L. McLean, Quinnipiac College; Lawrence W. Miller, Collin County Community College; Francie Mizell, Dekalb College; William J. Murin, University of Wisconsin–Parkside; Dale A. Neuman, University of Missouri–Kansas City; G. R. Patterson, Porterville College; Kelly D. Patterson, Brigham Young University; Richard Pride, Vanderbilt University; Ron Rapoport, College of William and Mary; James Reed, College of St. Benedict; William Rosburg, Kirkwood Community College; Ralph Salmi, California State University–San Bernadino; David Schultz, University of Minnesota; Randy Siefkin, Modesto Jr. College; Valerie Simms, Northeastern University; J. Donald Smith, Cornell College; Joseph Stewart, University of New Mexico; Christopher Stream, University of Idaho; Eric Uslaner, University of Maryland–College Park; Jeff Walz, Concordia University–Wisconsin; Robert Weber, St. John's University; Matthew E. Wetstein, San Joaquin Delta College; Peter Wielhouwer, Spelman College; Harvey Williams, Christopher Newport College; Nancy Zingale, University of St. Thomas; Gary Zuk, Auburn University.

PREFACE

The purpose of *American Government: An Introduction Using MicroCase ExplorIt* is to let you discover many basic aspects of the American government and political system for yourself. There is nothing make-believe or "only educational" about this package. You will have access to the highest-quality data files available to professional researchers. The "facts" you discover are not someone's opinion—they accurately describe the real world.

You will browse the best and latest information available on questions such as:

◆ To what extent is regionalism still a factor in American politics? Does the old "Solid South" still exist?

◆ To what extent are Americans interested in (and informed about) politics? What kinds of people are more interested and informed?

◆ Who participates in politics? What kinds of people are more likely to vote? Are nonvoters different from voters in terms of political views?

◆ In comparison with people in other nations, to what extent do Americans support civil liberties and civil rights? Would most Americans allow atheists or others who hold unpopular views to express those views? How many would be willing to vote for a woman for president?

◆ How do political parties function? How do Americans become party members? How are third parties handicapped in the United States?

◆ How does federalism work and why do people in some regions think it is unfair?

◆ What kinds of people are elected to Congress? Where do they get their money? Does it make any difference whether a member of Congress is a Democrat or a Republican? Are members of Congress more ideological or less ideological than the general public?

◆ What are minority presidents and how do they get elected? Why have so many presidents come from Ohio?

Discovering answers to these questions won't hurt a bit, even if you have never used a computer. The software is so easy to use that you will pick up everything you need to know in a few minutes.

What's New in the Seventh Edition

As before, the data sets are extensive, current, and from the best sources available. The seventh edition includes an even greater variety of data from the 1998 American National Election Study and the 1998 General Social Survey. We have added a substantial amount of information for the 106th Congress, including many important votes on bills. We have also updated much of the data for the 50 states, and we have added some entirely new data as well. The presidency file now covers all 43 presidents and includes the 2000 electoral college and popular vote.

As before, the ExplorIt software can be run in Windows directly from the CD-ROM without any installation required. However, if you prefer to install ExplorIt on your computer rather than running it directly from the CD-ROM, you still have this option.

GETTING STARTED

INTRODUCTION

Political science is an empirical science. The goal of this workbook is to help you learn how to use data to explore the world of political science and how to investigate new ideas and conduct research to test these ideas.

Each exercise in this workbook has two sections. The first section discusses a particular area of American government and demonstrates how data are used to support, augment, and test the ideas proposed. It is possible to read this section without using your computer. However, all of the graphics in the text can be created on your computer by following the ExplorIt Guide, which is described below. Ask your instructor whether you should follow along the first section of each exercise with a computer.

The worksheet section allows you to follow up on these ideas by doing your own research. You will use the student version of ExplorIt to complete these worksheets.

When you finish this workbook, you'll know what political scientists actually do!

SYSTEM REQUIREMENTS

- Windows 95 (or higher)

- 8 MB RAM

- CD-ROM drive

- 3.5" disk drive

- 15 MB of hard drive space (if you want to install it)

NETWORK VERSIONS OF STUDENT EXPLORIT

A network version of Student ExplorIt is available at no charge to instructors who adopt this book for their course. It's worth noting that Student ExplorIt can be run directly from the CD and diskette on virtually any computer network—regardless of whether a network version of Student ExplorIt has been installed.

INSTALLING STUDENT EXPLORIT

If you will be running Student ExplorIt directly from the CD-ROM and diskette—or if you will be using a version of Student ExplorIt that is installed on a network—skip to the section "Starting Student ExplorIt."

To install Student ExplorIt to a hard drive, you will need the diskette and CD-ROM that are packaged inside the back cover of this book. Then follow these steps in order:

1. Start your computer and wait until the Windows desktop is showing on your screen.

2. Insert the diskette into the A drive (or B drive) of your computer.

3. Insert the CD-ROM disc into the CD-ROM drive of your computer.

4. On most computers the CD-ROM will automatically start and a welcome menu will appear. If the CD-ROM doesn't automatically start, do the following:

    Click [Start] from the Windows desktop, click [Run], type **D:\SETUP**, and click [OK]. (If your CD-ROM drive is not the D drive, replace the letter D with the proper drive letter.)

5. To install Student ExplorIt to your hard drive, select the second option on the list: "Install Student ExplorIt to your hard drive."

6. During the installation, you will be presented with several screens, as described below. In most cases you will be required to make a selection or entry and then click [Next] to continue.

The first screen that appears is the **License Name** screen. (If this software has been previously installed or used, it already contains the licensing information. In such a case, a screen confirming your name will appear instead.) Here you are asked to type your name. It is important to type your name correctly, since it cannot be changed after this point. Your name will appear on all printouts, so make sure you spell it completely and correctly! Then click [Next] to continue.

A **Welcome** screen now appears. This provides some introductory information and suggests that you shut down any other programs that may be running. Click [Next] to continue.

You are next presented with a **Software License Agreement**. Read this screen and click [Yes] if you accept the terms of the software license.

The next screen has you **Choose the Destination** for the program files. You are strongly advised to use the destination directory that is shown on the screen. Click [Next] to continue.

The Student ExplorIt program will now be installed. At the end of the installation, you will be asked if you would like a shortcut icon placed on the Windows desktop. It is recommended that you select [Yes]. You are now informed that the installation of Student ExplorIt is finished. Click the [Finish] button and you will be returned to the opening Welcome Screen. To exit completely, click the option "Exit Welcome Screen."

INSTALLING STUDENT EXPLORIT TO A LAPTOP COMPUTER

If you are installing Student ExplorIt to a hard drive on a laptop that has both a CD-ROM drive and a floppy disk drive, simply follow the preceding instructions. However, if you are installing Student ExplorIt to a hard drive on a laptop where you cannot have both the CD-ROM drive and floppy disk drive attached at the same time, follow these steps in order:

1. Attach the CD-ROM drive to your computer and insert the CD-ROM disc.

2. Start your computer and wait until the Windows desktop is showing on your screen.

3. On most computers the CD-ROM will automatically start and a welcome menu will appear. If it does, click Exit.

4. Click [Start] from the Windows desktop, select [Programs], and select [Windows Explorer].

5. Click the drive letter for your CD-ROM in the left column (usually D:\). A list of folders and files on the CD-ROM will appear in the left column.

6. From the Windows Explorer menu, click [Edit] and [Select All]. The folders and files on the CD-ROM will be highlighted. Using your mouse, right click (use your right mouse button) on the list of folders and files. From the box that appears select [Copy].

7. In the left column of the Windows Explorer menu, right click once on your C drive (do NOT select a folder) and select [Paste] from the box that appears.

8. Close Windows Explorer by clicking the [X] button on the top right corner.

9. Remove the CD-ROM and CD-ROM drive from your computer and attach the floppy disk drive. Place the floppy disk drive from your workbook in the drive.

10. Click [Start] from the Windows desktop, click [Run], type C:\SETUP and click [OK].

11. Select the first option from the Welcome menu: **Run Student ExplorIt from the CD-ROM**. Within a few seconds Student ExplorIt will appear on your screen.

STARTING STUDENT EXPLORIT

There are three ways to run Student ExplorIt: (1) directly from the CD-ROM and diskette, (2) from a hard drive installation, or (3) from a network installation. Each method is described below.

Starting Student ExplorIt from the CD-ROM and Diskette

Unlike most Windows programs, it is possible to run Student ExplorIt directly from the CD-ROM and diskette. To do so, follow these steps:

1. Insert the 3.5" diskette into the A or B drive of your computer.

2. Insert the CD-ROM disc into the CD-ROM drive.

3. On most computers the CD-ROM will automatically start and a welcome menu will appear. (Note: If the CD-ROM does **not** automatically start after it is inserted, click [Start] from the Windows desktop, click [Run], type D:\SETUP and click [OK]. If your CD-ROM drive is not the D drive, replace the letter D with the proper drive letter.)

4. Select the first option from the Welcome menu: **Run Student ExplorIt from the CD-ROM**. Within a few seconds Student ExplorIt will appear on your screen.

Starting Student ExplorIt from a Hard Drive Installation

If Student ExplorIt is installed to the hard drive of your computer (see earlier section "Installing Student ExplorIt"), it is **not** necessary to insert either the CD-ROM or floppy diskette. Instead, locate the Student ExplorIt "shortcut" icon on the Windows desktop, which looks something like this:

To start Student ExplorIt, position your mouse pointer over the shortcut icon and double-click (that is, click it twice in rapid succession). If you did not permit the shortcut icon to be placed on the desktop during the install process (or if the icon was accidentally deleted), you can alternatively follow these directions to start the software:

Click [Start] from the Windows desktop.

Click [Programs].

Click MicroCase.

Click Student ExplorIt.

After a few seconds, Student ExplorIt will appear on your screen.

Starting Student ExplorIt from a Network

If the network version of Student ExplorIt has been installed to a computer network, you must insert the floppy diskette (not the CD-ROM) that comes with your book. Then double-click the Student ExplorIt icon that appears on the Windows desktop to start the program. (Note: Your instructor may provide additional information that is unique to your computer network.)

MAIN MENU OF STUDENT EXPLORIT

Student ExplorIt is extremely easy to use. All you do is point and click your way through the program. That is, use your mouse arrow to point at the selection you want, then click the left button on the mouse.

The main menu is the starting point for everything you will do in Student ExplorIt. Look at how it works. Notice that not all options on the menu are always available. You will know which options are available at any given time by looking at the colors of the options. For example, when you first start the software, only the OPEN FILE option is immediately available. As you can see, the colors for this option are brighter than those for the other tasks shown on the screen. Also, when you move your mouse pointer over this option, it is highlighted.

EXPLORIT GUIDES

Throughout this workbook, "ExplorIt Guides" provide the basic information needed to carry out each task. Here is an example:

➤ *Data File:* **STATES**
➤ *Task:* **Mapping**
➤ *Variable 1:* **116) MURDER**
➤ *View:* **Map**

Each line of the ExplorIt Guide is actually an instruction. Let's follow the simple steps to carry out this task.

Step 1: Select a Data File

Before you can do anything in Student ExplorIt, you need to open a data file. To open a data file, click the OPEN FILE task. A list of data files will appear in a window (e.g., COLONIAL, COUNTY, GSS, etc.). If you click on a file name *once*, a description of the highlighted file is shown in the window next to this list. In the ExplorIt Guide shown above, the ➤ symbol to the left of the Data File step indicates that you should open the STATES data file. To do so, click STATES and then click the [Open] button (or just double-click STATES). The next window that appears (labeled File Settings) provides additional information about the data file, including a file description, the number of cases in the file, and the number of variables, among other things. To continue, click the [OK] button. You are now returned to the main menu of Student ExplorIt. (You won't need to repeat this step until you want to open a different data file.) Notice that you can always see which data file is currently open by looking at the file name shown on the top line of the screen.

Step 2: Select a Task

Once you open a data file, the next step is to select a program task. Seven analysis tasks are offered in this version of Student ExplorIt. Not all tasks are available for each data file, because some tasks are appropriate only for certain kinds of data. Mapping, for example, is a task that applies only to ecological data, and thus cannot be used with survey data files.

In the ExplorIt Guide we're following, the ➤ symbol on the second line indicates that the MAPPING task should be selected, so click the MAPPING option with your left mouse button.

Step 3: Select a Variable

After a task is selected, you will be shown a list of the variables in the open data file. Notice that the first variable is highlighted and a description of that variable is shown in the Variable Description window at the lower right. You can move this highlight through the list of variables by using the up and down cursor keys (as well as the <Page Up> and <Page Down> keys). You can also click once on a variable name to move the highlight and update the variable description. Go ahead—move the highlight to a few other variables and read their descriptions.

If the variable you want to select is not showing in the variable window, click on the scroll bars located on the right side of the variable list window to move through the list. See the following figure:

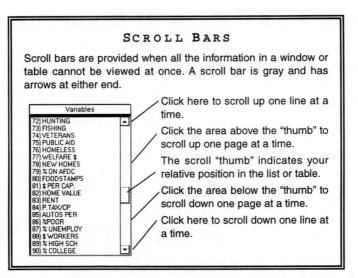

SCROLL BARS

Scroll bars are provided when all the information in a window or table cannot be viewed at once. A scroll bar is gray and has arrows at either end.

Click here to scroll up one line at a time.

Click the area above the "thumb" to scroll up one page at a time.

The scroll "thumb" indicates your relative position in the list or table.

Click the area below the "thumb" to scroll down one page at a time.

Click here to scroll down one line at a time.

By the way, you will find an appendix at the back of this workbook that contains a list of the variable names for key data files provided in this package.

Each task requires the selection of one or more variables, and the ExplorIt Guides indicate which variables should be selected. The ExplorIt Guide example here indicates that you should select 116) MURDER as Variable 1. On the screen, there is a box labeled Variable 1. Inside this box, there is a vertical cursor that indicates that this box is currently an active option. When you select a variable, it will be placed in this box. Before selecting a variable, be sure that the cursor is in the appropriate box. If it is not, place the cursor inside the appropriate box by clicking the box with your mouse. This is important because in some tasks the ExplorIt Guide will require more than one variable to be selected, and you want to be sure that you put each selected variable in the right place.

To select a variable, use any one of the methods shown below. (Note: If the name of a previously selected variable is in the box, use the <Delete> or <Backspace> key to remove it—or click the [Clear All] button.)

- Type the **number** of the variable and press <Enter>.

- Type the **name** of the variable and press <Enter>. Or you can type just enough of the name to distinguish it from other variables in the data—MUR would be sufficient for this example.

- Double-click the desired variable in the variable list window. This selection will then appear in the variable selection box. (If the name of a previously selected variable is in the box, the newly selected variable will replace it.)

- Highlight the desired variable in the variable list, then click the arrow that appears to the left of the variable selection box. The variable you selected will now appear in the box. (If the name of a previously selected variable is in the box, the newly selected variable will replace it.)

Once you have selected your variable (or variables), click the [OK] button to continue to the final results screen.

Step 4: Select a View

The next screen that appears shows the final results of your analysis. In most cases, the screen that first appears matches the "view" indicated in the ExplorIt Guide. In this example, you are instructed to look at the Map view—that's what is currently showing on the screen. In some instances, however, you may need to make an additional selection to produce the desired screen.

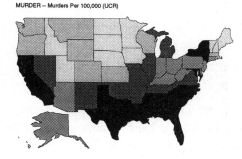

MURDER -- Murders Per 100,000 (UCR)

(OPTIONAL) Step 5: Select an Additional Display

Some ExplorIt Guides will indicate that an additional "Display" should be selected. In that case, simply click on the option indicated for that additional display. For example, this ExplorIt Guide may have included an additional line that required you to select the Legend display.

Step 6: Continuing to the Next ExplorIt Guide

Some instructions in the ExplorIt Guide may be the same for at least two examples in a row. For instance, after you display the map for murder in the example above, the following ExplorIt Guide may be given:

> Data File: **STATES**
> Task: **Mapping**
> ➤ Variable 1: **115) VIOL.CRIME**
> ➤ View: **Map**

Notice that the first two lines in the ExplorIt Guide do not have the ➤ symbol located in front of the items. That's because you already have the data file STATES open and you have already selected the MAPPING task. With the results of your first analysis showing on the screen, there is no need to return to the main menu to complete this next analysis. Instead, all you need to do is select VIOL.CRIME as your new variable. Click the [[⟲]] button located in the top left corner of your screen and the variable selection screen for the MAPPING task appears again. Replace the variable with 115) VIOL.CRIME and click [OK].

To repeat: You need to do only those items in the ExplorIt Guide that have the ➤ symbol in front of them. If you start from the top of the ExplorIt Guide, you're simply wasting your time.

If the ExplorIt Guide instructs you to select an entirely new task or data file, you will need to return to the main menu. To return to the main menu, simply click the [Menu] button located at the top left corner of the screen. At this point, select the new data file and/or task that is indicated in the ExplorIt Guide.

That's all there is to the basic operation of Student ExplorIt. Just follow the instructions given in the ExplorIt Guide and point and click your way through the program.

ON-LINE HELP

Student ExplorIt offers extensive on-line help. You can obtain task-specific help by pressing <F1> at any point in the program. For example, if you are performing a scatterplot analysis, you can press <F1> to see the help for the SCATTERPLOT task.

If you prefer to browse through a list of the available help topics, select **Help** from the pull-down menu at the top of the screen and select the **Help Topics** option. At this point, you will be provided a list of topic areas. Each topic is represented by a closed-book icon. To see what information is available in a given topic area, double-click on a book to "open" it. (For this version of the software, use only the "Student ExplorIt" section of help; do not use the "Student MicroCase" section.) When you double-click on a book graphic, a list of help topics is shown. A help topic is represented by a graphic with a piece of paper with a question mark on it. Double-click on a help topic to view it.

If you have questions about Student ExplorIt, try the on-line help described above. If you are not very familiar with software or computers, you may want to ask a classmate or your instructor for assistance.

EXITING FROM STUDENT EXPLORIT

If you are continuing to the next section of this workbook, it is *not* necessary to exit from Student ExplorIt quite yet. But when you are finished using the program, it is very important that you properly exit the software—do not just walk away from the computer or remove your diskette. To exit Student ExplorIt, return to the main menu and select the [Exit Program] button that appears on the screen.

Important: If you inserted your diskette and/or CD-ROM disc before starting Student ExplorIt, remember to remove it before leaving the computer.

Part I

FOUNDATIONS

America has always been a large and very diverse place—even before it became a nation.

In 1776, at the start of the American Revolution, the 13 colonies covered 4 times the area of France and 17 times the area of England—of all European nations at that time, only Russia had a greater land area. And, although the total population of the 13 colonies was a bit less than 4 million, that was not a small population for the time. The population of England then was only slightly more than 7 million and was concentrated in an area about the size of Pennsylvania, while the American colonists were spread across an extremely diverse range of climates and terrains. Moreover, the American people themselves differed greatly from one place to another, from mountaineers and merchants to sailors and slaves.

Thus, from the very start, the physical and human features of the United States have posed political challenges. How can such a large and diverse society be governed fairly, effectively, and democratically? More than two centuries of efforts to solve these fundamental questions provide the foundations of the American government.

In the first three exercises, you will explore aspects of these foundations.

EXERCISE 1

"ONE NATION": THE HISTORY AND POLITICS OF REGION

I pledge allegiance to the flag of the United States of America and to the Republic for which it stands, one Nation . . .

THE PLEDGE OF ALLEGIANCE,
FRANCIS BELLAMY, 1892

Tasks: Mapping, Historical Trends
Data Files: COLONIAL, STATES, COUNTY, HISTORY

In the beginning the "United States" were hardly united in any important sense of the word. Initially each "state" was a British colony administered independently by a governor and other officials sent from Britain. Even the perils of the Revolutionary War did not bring much unity. General George Washington often lacked troops and supplies because individual colonies often failed to keep their promises to provide them. Following the war, efforts to create a nation initially resulted in a very weak union of the 13 "states" under the provisions of the Articles of Confederation. The Articles established a national legislature having one house to which states could send up to seven delegates, but each state had only one vote. There was no president, and each state had its own courts. Real power remained in the individual states, and the national legislature was able to do very little. However, a series of political and economic crises led to growing support for a stronger central government. Eventually this resulted in the Constitutional Convention, which gathered in Philadelphia in 1787 and created the federal system that has been in operation since the Constitution was ratified by the states—Rhode Island being the last state to do so, on May 29, 1790.

All things considered, it was relatively easy to merge the original 13 colonies into a nation because they were similar in so many ways. For example, the overwhelming majority of citizens in each state were native English speakers of British ancestry (English, Scottish, Welsh, and Irish).

In a standard textbook, a statement like this might be followed by an instruction directing you to look at a printed map to show you the percentage of the population of British ancestry in each of the colonies. In fact, such a map appears on the next page of this book. But what makes this workbook different from an ordinary textbook is that *you* are able to generate a map of *any* item included in the COLONIAL, NATIONS, COUNTY, or STATES data files—whether it be a map of British ancestry in the American colonies or of the number of cocaine addicts per 1,000 population in the 50 states. And once a map is on your computer screen you can do a lot of other things to it, which you will discover as you proceed through this exercise.

➤ *Data File:* **COLONIAL**
➤ *Task:* **Mapping**
➤ *Variable 1:* **3) %BRITISH**
➤ *View:* **Map**

%BRITISH -- 1790: Percent of White Population of British Ancestry

> If you want to reproduce this graphic on the computer screen using ExplorIt, review the instructions in the *Getting Started* section. For this example, you would open the COLONIAL data file, select the MAPPING task, and select 3) %BRITISH for Variable 1. The first view shown is the Map view. (Remember, the ➤ symbol indicates which steps you need to perform if you are doing all examples as you follow along in the text. So in the next example, you only need to select a new view—that is, you don't need to repeat the first three steps because they were already done in this example.)

In this map of the nation in 1790, the states appear in several colors from very dark to very light. The darker a state, the higher the percentage of its citizens who were of British ancestry. The states shown in the lightest color have the lowest percentage. Now let's look at the actual percentages.

Data File: **COLONIAL**
Task: **Mapping**
Variable 1: **3) %BRITISH**
➤ *View:* **List: Rank**

RANK	CASE NAME	VALUE
1	Massachusetts	89.0
2	North Carolina	86.5
3	Virginia	84.9
4	South Carolina	84.7
5	Georgia	84.4
6	Vermont	84.3
7	Rhode Island	78.8
8	Maryland	77.9
9	Delaware	74.3
10	Maine	72.5

> As indicated by the ➤ symbol, if you are continuing from the previous example, select the [List: Rank] button. The number of rows shown on your screen may be different from that shown here. Use the cursor keys and scroll bar to move through this list if necessary.

Massachusetts was the highest, with 89 percent of its population in 1790 being of British ancestry. North Carolina was number two (86.5 percent). Moving down this list we discover that Pennsylvania was the lowest, but even it had a substantial majority (54.9 percent) of British origins. Let's note that there were many colonists from other nationalities as well, such as the French, the Germans, the Swedish, and the Dutch. Further, keep in mind that there were parts of the continent that were later to become part of the United States that were heavily French or Spanish (e.g., Louisiana, Florida). Keep in mind also that a substantial percentage of the population consisted of slaves, who were, of course, from Africa. However, the important point here is that the population of the original thirteen colonies was primarily from a British background and this had a great impact on the prospects of establishing a unified nation with a national identity.

4   *Part I: Foundations*

Political scientists frequently refer to "variables" when they do research. For example, they might describe the percent British as an "interesting variable." A **variable** is anything that varies or takes different values among the things or units of analysis being studied. In this case these things or units are the states in 1790. And the percent British is something that varies among them. But not just any feature of states is a variable. For example, each of the states had a population. Therefore, having a population is not a variable (it does not vary). But a different number of people lived in each state, and therefore the size of each state's population is a variable: We can rank states from the smallest to the largest. Similarly, the population of each state differed (or varied) in terms of what percentage of the total was of British ancestry. Other pertinent variables include the geography and climate of these states, their histories, the percentage who belonged to churches, the size of the average farm, and the number of bars and taverns per 10,000 population—all characteristics on which the states differ are variables.

When we study individuals, we also are interested in variables: age, sex, race, weight, education, income, party affiliation, favorite TV shows, and so on—all the ways in which people differ from one another are variables.

Sometimes political scientists seek variables that reveal the greatest amount of difference. However, for the moment, our interest is in showing that there was little variation among the original states on some variables, that in these ways the states were very similar. So let's examine another such variable.

% PROT. -- 1776: Percent of Church Members Who Are Protestants

Data File: **COLONIAL**
Task: **Mapping**
➤ Variable 1: **4) % PROT.**
➤ View: **Map**

If you are continuing from the previous example, use the [⟲] button to return to the variable selection screen. Select variable 4) % PROT. as the new Variable 1.

This map shows the percentage of all church members in each state who were Protestants in 1776.

Data File: **COLONIAL**
Task: **Mapping**
Variable 1: **4) % PROT.**
➤ View: **List: Rank**

RANK	CASE NAME	VALUE
1	Massachusetts	100.0
1	South Carolina	100.0
1	New Hampshire	100.0
1	Rhode Island	100.0
1	North Carolina	100.0
1	Connecticut	100.0
1	Maine	100.0
1	Vermont	100.0
1	Georgia	100.0
10	Virginia	99.8

The states were even more similar in terms of religion than ethnicity. In only six states were there any Roman Catholics, and even Maryland, initially the only colony that admitted Catholics, was overwhelmingly Protestant (84.4 percent). In fact, the great majority of Americans of Irish ancestry were Irish Protestants; it was not until the 1840s that substantial numbers of Irish Catholics began to arrive.

While the overwhelming majority of the colonists were Protestants, there was substantial diversity among these Protestants—a diversity that had strong implications for the development of the new nation and its Constitution and continues to be important in American politics today. "Protestantism" in the colonies ranged from Puritans to Methodists to a rational religion based on ideas coming out of European Enlightenment. Nevertheless, the common Protestant background helped to forge a coalition of traditional and nontraditional religious groups to carry out the American Revolution.

However, the original states were extremely different in one important way—a difference that would long haunt American political history: slavery.

Data File: **COLONIAL**
Task: **Mapping**
➤ Variable 1: **5) # SLAVES**
➤ View: **Map**

SLAVES -- 1790: Number of Slaves

Here the variable is the number of slaves in each state as recorded by the first U.S. Census, conducted in 1790.

Data File: **COLONIAL**
Task: **Mapping**
Variable 1: **5) # SLAVES**
➤ View: **List: Rank**

RANK	CASE NAME	VALUE
1	Virginia	293427
2	South Carolina	107094
3	Maryland	103036
4	North Carolina	100572
5	Georgia	29264
6	New York	21324
7	New Jersey	11423
8	Delaware	8887
9	Pennsylvania	3737
10	Connecticut	2759

Virginia had 293,427 slaves in 1790 (out of a total population of 748,308). South Carolina was second with 107,094. However, in 1790 slavery was not restricted to the southern states. In 1774 Rhode Island was the first colony to abolish slavery, but did not free those currently in bondage, requiring only that their children be born free (which is why in 1790 there were still 952 slaves in Rhode Island). In 1780 Massachusetts outlawed slavery with no exemptions, which is why no slaves were found in that state by the time of the first census (at that time Maine was part of Massachusetts). That same year

Pennsylvania abolished slavery but exempted current slaves, which is why there still were 3,737 slaves in 1790. Connecticut abolished slavery, with exemptions, in 1784. Notice that there were many slaves in New York and New Jersey in 1790. That's because these states did not outlaw slavery until 1799 and 1820, respectively. All importation of slaves into the United States was prohibited by federal law in 1808, but it would take a civil war to free the slaves already here.

As new states came into the Union, repeated battles arose as to whether slavery would be legal or prohibited in each. The first severe conflict arose in 1820 when Missouri applied for statehood as a "slave" state. Because that would have created a majority in the Senate from states permitting slavery, Missouri's admission was opposed by northern senators. The "Missouri Compromise" admitted Missouri as a slave state, but balanced its Senate membership by at the same time admitting Maine as a "free" state. The compromise also drew a line across the nation and proposed that in the future all new territory north of this line would be free and all south of it slave. This line, just south of the border between Pennsylvania and Maryland, was known as the Mason-Dixon line. The compromise did not last and, as the nation expanded westward, conflicts over slavery grew increasingly heated.

➤ *Data File:* **STATES**
➤ *Task:* **Mapping**
➤ *Variable 1:* **9) SLAVE/FREE**
➤ *View:* **Map**

SLAVE/FREE -- 1860: Slave States = Dark; Free States = Light

The ➤ symbol on the Data File line indicates that you must return to the main menu and open a new data file—STATES.

In 1860, 15 states did not yet exist, so these states were neither slave nor free. Since these states have no data, they are the same color as the background on this map. On the ranking screen, the value of this variable for each of these states will be blank. West Virginia was part of Virginia prior to the Civil War and is shown as a slave state on this map.

Here the variable shows the split between slave and free states in 1860. Fifteen states had slavery, 19 states were free: The balance had been tipped by the admission of Kansas, Oregon, and California as free states. No wonder that the future of slavery became the dominant issue in the 1860 presidential election. There were four major candidates. First to be nominated was John Bell of Tennessee, running as the candidate of the Constitutional Union Party, which took a moderate stand on slavery. The second was Abraham Lincoln, the nominee of the new, antislavery Republican Party. That year the Democratic Party split over the issue of slavery, the southern faction adopting a platform supporting the right to own slaves while the northern faction took a much more circumspect position on the issue. The northern faction nominated Stephen A. Douglas for president, and the southern Democrats chose John C. Breckinridge of Kentucky, the current vice president. As the campaign developed and slavery became the main issue, many southern leaders made it clear that the South would secede if Lincoln won.

Data File: **STATES**
Task: **Mapping**
Variable 1: **9) SLAVE/FREE**
➤ Variable 2: **11) STATES1860**
➤ Views: **Map**

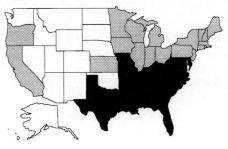

SLAVE/FREE -- 1860: Slave States = Dark; Free States = Light

STATES1860 -- 1860: Electoral Votes: Lincoln=Light;Douglas or Bell=Medium; Breckinridge=Dark

If you are continuing from the previous example, return to the variable selection screen. Keep 9) SLAVE/FREE selected as Variable 1 and select 11) STATES1860 as Variable 2.

Notice how similar these maps are. Lincoln won a close election by carrying 18 of the free states, some by very narrow margins (he won California by 711 votes out of a total of 119,868). Douglas took Missouri and New Jersey, Bell took Virginia, Kentucky, and Tennessee, and Breckinridge carried 11 slave states.

Data File: **STATES**
Task: **Mapping**
Variable 1: **9) SLAVE/FREE**
➤ Variable 2: **10) UNION/CONF**
➤ Views: **Map**

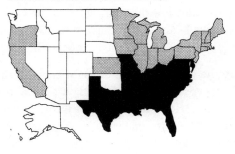

SLAVE/FREE -- 1860: Slave States = Dark; Free States = Light

8

UNION/CONF -- 1861: States of the Union = Light; of the Confederacy = Dark

If you are continuing from the previous example, replace Variable 2, 11) STATES1860, with 10) UNION/CONF.

Following Lincoln's election, the South made good on its threats to secede, South Carolina being the first to do so, and the Civil War ensued. This map shows the states that remained in the Union (light colored) and those that joined the Confederate States. (West Virginia split from Virginia in opposition to the Confederacy.) By the time the war ended, 444,964 soldiers (North and South) had died to determine whether this would be two nations or one. In fact, the Civil War was the bloodiest war in American history—407,316 Americans were killed in World War II, 116,708 in World War I, 58,168 in the Vietnam War, and 293 in the Gulf War.

Although the Civil War settled the issue of slavery, it did not resolve issues concerning the position of African Americans, especially in the South, and continuing concerns about race and bitter memories of the war shaped the politics of the South for the next century.

     Data File: **STATES**
        Task: **Mapping**
   Variable 1: **9) SLAVE/FREE**
➤ *Variable 2:* **81) STATES '20**
    ➤ *Views:* **Map**

SLAVE/FREE -- 1860: Slave States = Dark; Free States = Light

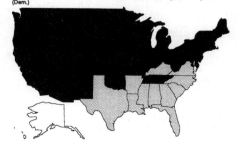

STATES '20 -- 1920: Dark States Carried by Harding (Rep.), Light States by Cox (Dem.)

The comparison map on the preceding page shows the results of the 1920 presidential election. Warren G. Harding, Republican U.S. senator from Ohio, ran against Ohio's Democratic governor, James M. Cox. Harding won a huge victory, receiving about 62 percent of the popular votes. But he failed to win any of the states that had belonged to the Confederacy. These 11 states gave all of their electoral votes to the Democratic candidate. In fact, the Republican candidate didn't even come close in these states— Harding received a minuscule 3.4 percent of the votes in South Carolina and only 14 percent in Mississippi.

Moreover, the South always gave this kind of support to Democratic candidates, holding Republicans responsible for Lincoln and the Civil War. As a result, for several generations, political commentators referred to "the Solid South," noting that every Democratic presidential candidate could count on these votes and could win by just breaking close to even elsewhere.

The Solid South began to soften during the years of the Eisenhower administration, and it appears that the 1960 presidential election was the last time that a non-southern Democratic presidential candidate could count on most of the old Solid South. The dark states on the following map are the ones carried by Kennedy, who did well in the South.

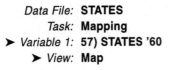

STATES '60 -- 1960: Dark States Carried by Kennedy (Dem.), Light Ones by Nixon (Rep.)

In the 1964 presidential election landslide, the Democratic candidate, Johnson, won all but six states, but five of these six states were in the South. Perhaps because Johnson steered the 1964 Civil Rights Act through Congress, he did worse in the South than in the rest of the country. Thus, the crumbling of the Solid South was evident in 1964. This crumbling continued in 1968 when the Democratic candidate, Humphrey, did worse in the South than anywhere else. The migration of southern voters to the Republican Party was not yet evident, however, because of the third-party candidacy of Alabama's George Wallace, who carried five southern states and received a substantial percentage of the votes in some other southern states.

The end of the Solid South was very evident in the 1972 election. Not only did the Republican candidate, Nixon, win by a landslide, but, as the following map shows, he did better in the South than anywhere else.

Data File: **STATES**
Task: **Mapping**
➤ *Variable 1:* **50) %NIXON '72**
➤ *View:* **Map**

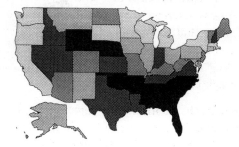

Notice that the majority of the darkest colored states, where Nixon received the largest percentage of the vote in 1972, are in the South.

Data File: **STATES**
Task: **Mapping**
Variable 1: **50) %NIXON '72**
➤ *View:* **List: Rank**

RANK	CASE NAME	VALUE
1	Mississippi	78.2
2	Georgia	75.3
3	Oklahoma	73.7
4	Alabama	72.4
5	Florida	71.9
6	South Carolina	70.8
7	Nebraska	70.5
8	North Carolina	69.5
9	Wyoming	69.0
10	Arkansas	68.9

Additional values may be scrolled on the screen.

In a year when he carried every state except Massachusetts, it was Mississippi that give Nixon his largest margin, followed by Georgia, Oklahoma, Alabama, Florida, and South Carolina.

Finally, the legacy of slavery was no longer the dominant feature of American regionalism. In that sense, we had moved closer to being "One Nation."

➤ *Data File:* **HISTORY**
➤ *Task:* **Historical Trends**
➤ *Variables:* **27) SOUTH.DEM**

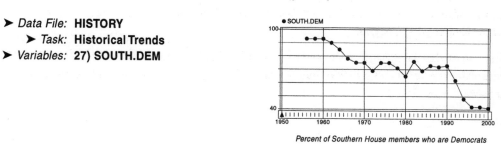

Percent of Southern House members who are Democrats

The ➤ symbol on the Data File line indicates that you must return to the main menu and open a new data file—HISTORY.

The percentage of southern members of the House who are Democrats has declined from over 90 percent in 1956 to only 41 percent after the 2000 elections.

While the Solid South is no more, the South is still a distinctive region.

> ➤ *Data File:* **STATES**
> ➤ *Task:* **Mapping**
> ➤ *Variable 1:* **8) THE SOUTH**
> ➤ *View:* **Map**

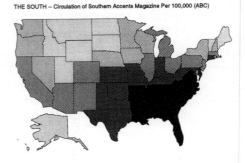

THE SOUTH -- Circulation of Southern Accents Magazine Per 100,000 (ABC)

Note that this task uses a new data file.

One way to isolate the remnants of southern allegiance is with the circulation rates of the magazine *Southern Accents*. While *Southern Accents* has subscribers in all 50 states, they are highly concentrated in the states of the Old South. Notice how similar the map of *Southern Accents* circulation is to the earlier map showing the states of the Union and the Confederacy during the Civil War.

Data File: **STATES**
Task: **Mapping**
Variable 1: **8) THE SOUTH**
➤ *View:* **List: Rank**

RANK	CASE NAME	VALUE
1	Georgia	385.2
2	Alabama	381.5
3	South Carolina	372.2
4	North Carolina	339.1
5	Tennessee	319.2
6	Mississippi	288.3
7	Virginia	283.7
8	Louisiana	247.2
9	Arkansas	206.1
10	Florida	197.6

Georgia has the highest circulation rate (385.2 copies per 100,000 population) closely followed by Alabama, the Carolinas, Tennessee, and Mississippi. Utah, the Dakotas, and Montana have the lowest rates.

Today, there are substantial African American populations in many states outside the South, especially in the more urban states. But the majority of African Americans still live in the South where they have become a very important political factor.

Data File: **STATES**
Task: **Mapping**
Variable 1: **8) THE SOUTH**
➤ Variable 2: **24) %AFRIC.AM**
➤ Views: **Map**

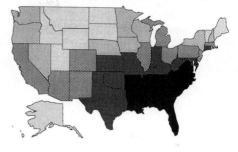

THE SOUTH -- Circulation of Southern Accents Magazine Per 100,000 (ABC)

%AFRIC.AM -- Percent African American 1998 (Census)

The South is only one region.

Data File: **STATES**
Task: **Mapping**
➤ Variable 1: **3) BIG REGION**
➤ View: **Map**

BIG REGION -- Large Regions As Defined by the Census

The Bureau of the Census defines the major American regions as the East, Midwest, South, and West. These regions are very useful for many purposes. States within a given region have certain historical and geographic similarities. But they fail to capture the real subtleties of American regionalism: that the nation consists of various regions depending on what is at issue.

Indeed, the famous analogy of the great American "melting pot" is somewhat of an exaggeration when one examines the regional variations that exist in terms of ethnicity, economics, and culture. Let's use a county-level data file to examine several race and ethnicity variables.

➤ *Data File:* **COUNTY**
　　➤ *Task:* **Mapping**
➤ *Variable 1:* **4) %BLACK**
　　➤ *View:* **Map**

%BLACK -- PERCENT BLACK (1990s)

The advantage of the county-level map is that it shows more details of the variations that exist across the nation. This map provides a county-level breakdown of the percentage of African Americans. As expected, the map is similar to the state-level map shown earlier in terms of the regions where African Americans are most populous (the South).

Let's see where the largest Hispanic populations are found.

Data File: **COUNTY**
Task: **Mapping**
➤ *Variable 1:* **6) %HISPANIC2**
➤ *View:* **Map**

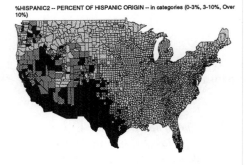

%HISPANIC2 -- PERCENT OF HISPANIC ORIGIN -- in categories (0-3%, 3-10%, Over 10%)

This map is very different. Here we see that people of Hispanic origin are more likely to live in the southwestern part of the United States. Counties with the darkest colors have Hispanic populations greater than 10 percent. (To examine the actual percentage for a given county, use variable %HISPANIC.)

Do American Indians tend to live in one region of the United States?

Data File: **COUNTY**
Task: **Mapping**
➤ *Variable 1:* **10) %AMER.IND2**
➤ *View:* **Map**

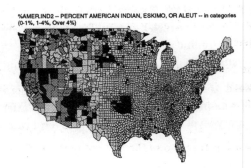

%AMER.IND2 -- PERCENT AMERICAN INDIAN, ESKIMO, OR ALEUT -- in categories (0-1%, 1-4%, Over 4%)

Whereas the South is widely populated by African Americans, and the Southwest has large percentages of people of Hispanic origin, American Indian populations tend to be concentrated in particular counties in Oklahoma, Arizona, and Nevada. In fact, there are many instances where a county having a high percentage of American Indians borders a county with a very low percentage of American Indians—this often reflects the location of Indian reservations.

In the worksheet section we will continue to examine regional differences in race and ethnicity. Another important way to view regional variation in America is to look at wealth and poverty rates. This time we'll analyze two maps at once.

> Data File: **COUNTY**
> Task: **Mapping**
> ➤ Variable 1: **19) %POOR**
> ➤ Variable 2: **20) MED.FAM$**
> ➤ Views: **Map**

%POOR -- PERCENT BELOW POVERTY LEVEL (1990s)

MED.FAM$ -- MEDIAN FAMILY MONEY INCOME (1990s)

An examination of the top map reveals that the highest levels of poverty occur in the Appalachian region and throughout much of the South. Notice that the poverty rates are particularly low in the Northeast and in portions of the Midwest. If you examine the ranked list for this map, you'll discover there are 130 counties in which at least one-third of the population live below the official poverty rate. By contrast, there are dozens of counties in which less than 5 percent of the population live below the poverty level. Clearly, there are significant differences in the United States in terms of wealth and poverty.

The bottom map displays the median family income for each county. Not surprisingly, this map is nearly the opposite of the top map. For instance, notice that the dark areas in the top map tend to be colored lightly in the bottom map, and vice versa.

Let's compare two more maps: one that shows the percentage of earnings that come from farming and the other that shows the percentage of earnings that come from manufacturing.

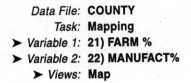

Data File: **COUNTY**
Task: **Mapping**
➤ Variable 1: **21) FARM %**
➤ Variable 2: **22) MANUFACT%**
➤ Views: **Map**

FARM % -- FARM SHARE (%) OF TOTAL EARNINGS (1990s)

MANUFACT% -- PERCENT OF EARNINGS FROM MANUFACTURING (1990s)

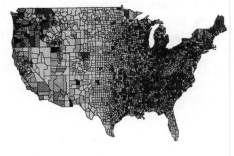

The distinctions between the farming and manufacturing regions of the United States are clear. People living in the central part of the country are more likely to rely on farming for income than are those living in the East. Likewise, people living in the East are more likely to be employed in manufacturing.

At the beginning of this exercise, we saw that it was the similarities of the early colonies that helped pave the way to nationhood. By the middle of the 19th century, it was regional differences among states that led to the Civil War. Today, there continue to be substantial social, cultural, and economic differences across the regions of the nation. But do these regional differences have political implications as they did in the past? Although these differences are unlikely to lead to civil war, they surely affect the way people vote, the laws and policies that are enacted at the state and local levels, the decisions that are made in courts, and so on.

For instance, it is likely that states with high percentages of families on public aid will be more concerned with issues that relate to social programs. Voters in states where family incomes are relatively high might be more responsive to political candidates who propose lower taxes on investment earnings. States with large percentages of people who speak a language other than English may be more concerned with laws relating to bilingual education and immigration. States with higher crime rates will be more concerned about crime-related issues. Indeed, regionalism is an important factor in American politics and it will be referred to often throughout this workbook.

Your turn.

Part I: Foundations

FEDERALISM: "A MORE PERFECT UNION"

> *We the People of the United States, in Order to form a more perfect Union, establish Justice, insure domestic Tranquility, provide for the common defence, promote the general Welfare, and secure the Blessings of Liberty to ourselves and our Posterity, do ordain and establish this Constitution for the United States of America.*
>
> PREAMBLE TO THE CONSTITUTION, SEPTEMBER 17, 1787

Tasks: Mapping, Scatterplot
Data File: STATES

From the start, Americans had two basic concerns about the structure of their government. First, they wished to retain as much local authority as possible—each state had its particular concerns, interests, and local culture that it wished to protect. Second, they wished to have sufficient centralized authority so as to regulate relations among the states and provide for the common interests—defense, for example. The first attempt failed—the Articles of Confederation maximized the independence of the states, but failed to provide sufficient central authority. So, the Constitutional Convention tried a different approach. The result was called **federalism**, a system of government wherein two or more levels of government have formal authority over the same geographic area and the same citizens. That is, unlike most European nations, which concentrate nearly all power in a central government, a great deal of power was reserved for local governments—state, county, and city. But, unlike the previous confederation, the federal government was given substantial powers to enforce laws and policies nationwide. These powers were specifically spelled out in the Constitution. In addition, the Bill of Rights, the first ten amendments to the Constitution that were adopted at the end of 1791, further specified limits on the powers of governments and noted:

Amendment X: Rights Reserved to the States

The powers not delegated to the United States by the Constitution, nor prohibited by it to the States, are reserved to the States respectively, or to the people.

Despite these provisions, the federal and local governments exist in a state of mutual tension, pulling and pushing for greater control. During the two centuries since the federal government was created, it has gained a great deal more power than was intended by those who drew up the Constitution and the power of the individual states has been curtailed.

In addition, the balance between the federal and local governments differs greatly from place to place. This is especially obvious when we examine the percentage of land in each state that is owned by the federal government.

> ➤ Data File: **STATES**
> ➤ Task: **Mapping**
> ➤ Variable 1: **17) %FED LAND**
> ➤ View: **Map**

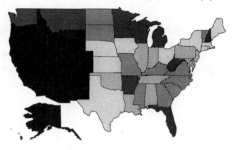

%FED LAND -- Percent of State's Area That Is Owned by the Federal Gov't. (SR)

If you want to reproduce this graphic on the computer screen using ExplorIt, review the instructions in the *Getting Started* section. For this example, you would open the STATES data file, select the MAPPING task, and select 17) %FED LAND for Variable 1. The first view shown is the Map view. (Remember, the ➤ symbol indicates which steps you need to perform if you are doing all examples as you follow along in the text. So in the next example, you only need to select a new view—that is, you don't need to repeat the first three steps because they were already done in this example.)

On this map, the darker a state, the larger the proportion of its area that consists of federally owned land.

> Data File: **STATES**
> Task: **Mapping**
> Variable 1: **17) %FED LAND**
> ➤ View: **List: Rank**

RANK	CASE NAME	VALUE
1	Nevada	82.74
2	Alaska	67.87
3	Utah	63.80
4	Idaho	61.72
5	Oregon	52.42
6	Wyoming	48.79
7	Arizona	47.10
8	California	44.45
9	Colorado	36.20
10	New Mexico	33.09

Nevada is highest: 82.7 percent of Nevada's land doesn't belong to Nevada at all, but to the federal government. That is, most of the area of the state is controlled by Congress and by federal agencies, and the residents of the state have very little say about how the land is used or regulated. In fact, the federal government can prohibit Nevadans from even entering parts of the state, as it often did from areas used for testing nuclear weapons. Alaska is second with two-thirds of its land under federal ownership. Utah (63.8 percent) is a very close third. Even in California, close to half (44.5 percent) of all land is federally owned. However, in many states Congress has little or no say in local land use because the amount of federal ownership is trivial: less than 1 percent in Connecticut, Rhode Island, New York, Maine, Kansas, and Iowa. For the 50 states, the average percentage of land owned by the federal government is 15 percent.

Data File: **STATES**
Task: **Mapping**
Variable 1: **17) %FED LAND**
➤ Variable 2: **7) THE WEST**
➤ Views: **Map**

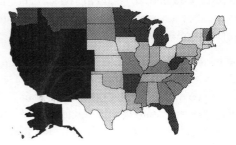

%FED LAND -- Percent of State's Area That Is Owned by the Federal Gov't. (SR)

r = 0.770**

THE WEST -- Degree of Longitude West of Prime Meridian Is Westernmost Point of State (except Alaska = Juneau)

If you are continuing from the previous example, return to the variable selection screen for the MAPPING task. Then select variable 7) THE WEST as Variable 2.

As is quite obvious, federal ownership of land is a very western phenomenon. As the last states to enter the Union, the western states always have faced a maximum amount of federal interference as Congress, controlled by the more populous eastern states, makes decisions based on easterners' preferences, not necessarily those of westerners. For example, Congress decides whether to permit western ranchers to graze their herds on federal land. Perhaps even more important, the eastern states have prevented the sale of federal lands in the West, defining much of it as protected wilderness areas. Many westerners complain that Congress never decides to turn large tracts of the East back into wilderness areas. These western resentments often show up rather clearly in elections and have been referred to as the "sagebrush revolt."

A source of friction inherent in federalism is over tax revenues, the proportion taken by the federal government versus the amount left to each state. This issue has been especially heated in recent times because the federal government often has initiated programs and then required each state to provide the funds. A similar friction persists at more local levels since each state is a mini-federal system wherein the state competes with local governments such as counties and cities for authority and funds.

Until the 16th Amendment to the Constitution was ratified in 1913, tax competition between the federal and state governments was minimized since each had its own separate sources. Until the 20th century, virtually all federal revenues came from customs duties on imports from abroad and from excise taxes on alcohol and tobacco, while state and local revenues came mainly from property taxes. There were neither federal nor state income taxes. During the Civil War the federal government imposed an income tax (with a minimum rate of 3 percent and a maximum rate of 5 percent). This tax was cancelled after the end of the war. In 1894 President Grover Cleveland, the newly elected

Democrat, pushed an income tax law through Congress. It was held to be unconstitutional by the Supreme Court, thus requiring backers of the tax to amend the Constitution (the 16th Amendment) in order to tax incomes. Begun in 1913, the federal income tax rates soon rose far beyond the "maximum limits" promised when the amendment was adopted.

The income tax facilitated a massive shift in governmental power because it provided the federal government with such an immense source of revenue. Thus, in 1900, prior to the income tax, state and local governments spent about twice as much per year as did the federal government. Today the federal government collects and spends about $2 to every $1 spent by state and local governments. And the income tax is the largest source of federal revenue. This is true despite the fact that in the latter part of the 20th century many states (now numbering 39) began collecting income taxes too.

INCOME TAX -- Federal Income Tax Per Capita, 1996 (Internal Revenue Service)

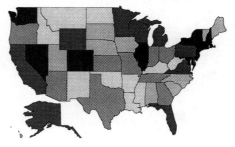

Data File:	**STATES**
Task:	**Mapping**
➤ Variable 1:	**20) INCOME TAX**
➤ View:	**Map**

Not surprisingly, the average resident in some states pays far more in federal income taxes than does the average resident in some other states.

Data File:	**STATES**
Task:	**Mapping**
Variable 1:	**20) INCOME TAX**
➤ View:	**List: Rank**

RANK	CASE NAME	VALUE
1	Connecticut	4517
2	New Jersey	3719
3	Massachusetts	3459
4	Nevada	3392
5	New York	3166
6	Illinois	3118
7	New Hampshire	3042
8	Maryland	2967
9	Washington	2893
10	Colorado	2890

The average person in Connecticut pays the most federal income tax ($4,517) per person, followed by residents of New Jersey ($3,719). People in Mississippi pay the least ($1,487), only one-third of what people in Connecticut pay. Now let's examine family incomes in the states.

Data File: **STATES**
Task: **Mapping**
➤ Variable 1: **13) FAMILY $**
➤ View: **Map**

FAMILY $ -- Median family income 1997 (SA, 1999)

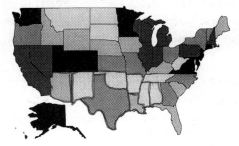

Data File: **STATES**
Task: **Mapping**
Variable 1: **13) FAMILY $**
➤ View: **List: Rank**

RANK	CASE NAME	VALUE
1	New Jersey	48021
2	Alaska	47994
3	Maryland	46685
4	Washington	44562
5	Connecticut	43985
6	Colorado	43233
7	Delaware	43033
8	Virginia	42957
9	Utah	42775
10	Minnesota	42564

No surprise. Connecticut and New Jersey also are among the states with the highest median family incomes and Mississippi is among the lowest here too.

Obviously, per capita income tax payments reflect income. States where people earn the most are states where people pay the most income tax. That is confirmed by this map of median family income, which closely resembles the map of per capita income taxes. And that statement raises this issue: How much alike must two maps be in order for them to be "alike"?

In Exercise 1 you were asked to compare many maps of the United States and to say which ones were very similar and which ones were very different. You no doubt found it easy to notice when two maps were very much alike. But, as you examined maps that were less alike, you must have found it more difficult to say how much alike they were.

As it turns out, there is a simple method for determining precisely how much alike are any two maps. It was invented about 100 years ago in England by Karl Pearson. Once you see how he did it, you will find it easy to apply.

Let's begin with these two maps of income taxes and family income.

To see Pearson's method, we can draw a horizontal line across the bottom of a piece of paper. We will let this line represent the map of median family income. So, at the left end of this line we will write 26,162, which indicates Arkansas, the state with the lowest income. At the right end of the line we will write 48,021 to represent New Jersey as the state with the highest income.

26,162   48,021

Now we can draw a vertical line up the left side of the paper. This line will represent the map of per capita income tax. At the bottom of this line we will write 1,487 to represent Mississippi, the state with the lowest income tax. At the top we will write 4,517 to represent Connecticut, the state with the highest income tax.

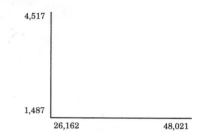

Now that we have a line with an appropriate scale to represent each map, the next thing we need to do is refer to the distributions for each map in order to learn the value for each state and then locate it on each line according to its score. Let's start with New Jersey. Since it is the state with the highest median income, we can easily find its place on the horizontal line. We will make a small mark at 48,021 to locate New Jersey. Next, New Jersey has a per capita federal income tax of $3,719. So, we make a mark on the vertical line about where we think that 3,719 would be. This point will be roughly three-fourths up the vertical line. Now we draw a line up from the mark for New Jersey on the horizontal line and draw another out from the mark for New Jersey on the vertical line. Where these two lines meet (or intersect), we draw a dot. This dot represents the combined map locations of New Jersey—it represents both the per capita income tax and the median family income for this state.

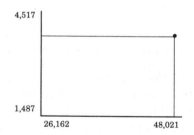

Now let's locate Connecticut. To find Connecticut on the horizontal line (also known as the X-axis), estimate where 43,985 is located and make a mark at that spot. Connecticut's tax rate is easy to find because it is the highest: 4,517. So, make a mark at 4,517 on the vertical line (also known as the Y-axis). Now we draw a line up from the horizontal line and draw another line across from the mark on the vertical line. Where these two lines intersect, we put a dot to represent Connecticut for both per capita income tax and median family income.

When we have followed this procedure for each state, we will have 50 dots located within the space defined by the vertical and horizontal lines representing the two maps. What we have done is to create a **scatterplot**. Fortunately, you don't have to go to all this trouble. ExplorIt will do it for you.

Data File: **STATES**
➤ Task: **Scatterplot**
➤ Dependent Variable: **20) INCOME TAX**
➤ Independent Variable: **13) FAMILY $**

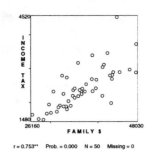

Notice that the SCATTERPLOT task requires two variables.

Special feature: When the scatterplot is showing, you may obtain information on any dot by clicking on it. A little box will appear around the dot, and the values of 13) FAMILY $ (or the X-axis variable) and of 20) INCOME TAX (or the Y-axis variable) will be shown.

Each of these dots is a state.

Once Pearson had created a scatterplot, his next step was to calculate what he called the **regression line**.

Data File: **STATES**
Task: **Scatterplot**
Dependent Variable: **20) INCOME TAX**
Independent Variable: **13) FAMILY $**
➤ View: **Reg. Line**

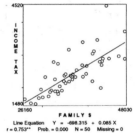

To show the regression line, select the [Reg. Line] option from the menu.

The regression line represents the best effort to draw a straight line that connects all of the dots. It is unnecessary for you to know how to calculate the location of the regression line—the program does it for you.

To see how the regression line would look if the maps were identical, all you need to do is examine the scatterplot for identical maps. So, if you create a scatterplot using FAMILY $ as both the dependent and independent variables, you will be comparing identical maps and the dots representing states will all be on the regression line like a string of beads.

However, since the maps for income tax and income are only very similar, but not identical, most of the dots are scattered near, but not on, the regression line. Pearson's method for calculating how much alike are any two maps or lists is easy, once the regression line has been drawn. What it amounts to is measuring the distance out from the regression line to every dot.

<table>
<tr><td align="right">Data File:</td><td>**STATES**</td></tr>
<tr><td align="right">Task:</td><td>**Scatterplot**</td></tr>
<tr><td align="right">Dependent Variable:</td><td>**20) INCOME TAX**</td></tr>
<tr><td align="right">Independent Variable:</td><td>**13) FAMILY $**</td></tr>
<tr><td align="right">➤ View:</td><td>**Reg. Line/Residuals**</td></tr>
</table>

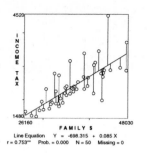

To show the residuals, select the [Residuals] option from the menu.

See all the little lines. If you added them all together, you would have a sum of the deviation of the dots from the regression line. The smaller this sum, the more alike are the two maps. For example, when the maps are identical and all the dots are on the regression line, the sum of the deviations is 0.

In order to make it simple to interpret results, Pearson invented a procedure to convert the sums into a number he called the **correlation coefficient**. The correlation coefficient varies from 0.0 to 1.0. When maps are identical, the correlation coefficient will be 1.0. When they are completely unalike, the correlation coefficient will be 0.0. Thus, the closer the correlation coefficient is to 1.0, the more alike the two maps or lists. Pearson used the letter r as the symbol for his correlation coefficient.

Look at the lower left of the screen above and you will see r = 0.753. This indicates that the maps are extremely similar. (The meaning of the asterisks will be explained a bit later.)

Correlation coefficients can be either positive or negative. This correlation is positive: Where incomes are higher, people pay higher income taxes. That is, as one rises so does the other—they tend to occur in unison. But when we examine a new scatterplot, the whole picture changes radically.

<table>
<tr><td align="right">Data File:</td><td>**STATES**</td></tr>
<tr><td align="right">Task:</td><td>**Scatterplot**</td></tr>
<tr><td align="right">➤ Dependent Variable:</td><td>**12) MOBILE HOM**</td></tr>
<tr><td align="right">➤ Independent Variable:</td><td>**20) INCOME TAX**</td></tr>
<tr><td align="right">➤ View:</td><td>**Reg. Line**</td></tr>
</table>

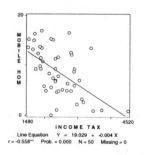

Here we see that where per capita income tax payments are lower, the higher the percentage who live in mobile homes. Notice that in this case the regression line slopes downward from left to right, rather than upward. That always indicates a negative correlation. And notice that a minus sign now precedes the correlation coefficient: r = −0.558.

The point of calculating correlation coefficients is not simply to say how alike or unalike two maps are. Indeed, the point of comparing two maps usually is not motivated by artistic concerns, but is done in search of links, or connections, between variables. In Exercise 1 you looked for links between regions and potential political issues. Moreover, only when such links exist can we propose that there is a causal relationship between them. Thus, implicit in our first two uses of the scatterplot technique was the assumption that one variable might be the cause of the other.

No one would really think it is just an accident that there is an extremely high correlation between income and income taxes. Rather, it seems likely that one is a cause of the other—that people must pay high income taxes because they have high incomes. In similar fashion, its seems likely that income tax rates are lower where more people live in mobile homes because people living in mobile homes tend to have lower incomes. In fact, we can check that out.

Data File: **STATES**
Task: **Scatterplot**
Dependent Variable: **12) MOBILE HOM**
➤ Independent Variable: **13) FAMILY $**
➤ View: **Reg. Line**

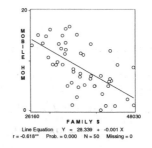

Once again we find a strong, negative correlation (r = –0.618). This tells us that where median family income is lower, more people live in mobile homes.

Whenever social scientists become interested in a variable, the first thing they generally ask is what causes it to vary. And the first test of any proposed answer to such a question is to demonstrate the existence of a correlation between the variable to be explained and its proposed cause. In this instance we have demonstrated that income may be a cause of the kind of housing people have since the two variables are highly correlated. By itself correlation does not establish that a causal relationship exists. But without a correlation, there can be no causal relationship between two variables.

That helps explain the distinction between independent and dependent variables. In the SCATTERPLOT task, the software first asks for the dependent variable and then asks for the independent variable. If we think something might be the cause of something else, then we say that the cause is the independent variable and that the consequence (or the thing being caused) is the dependent variable. Put another way, the dependent variable *depends on* the independent variable.

Now, suppose someone suggests that the prevalence of mobile homes has as much to do with climate as with income—that mobile homes are concentrated in the Sunbelt because of the mild weather. To test that suggestion we create another scatterplot.

Data File: **STATES**
Task: **Scatterplot**
Dependent Variable: **12) MOBILE HOM**
➤ Independent Variable: **6) SUNBELT**
➤ View: **Reg. Line**

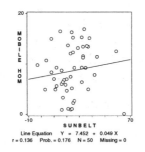

This is what a scatterplot looks like when two variables are not correlated. The dots are scattered all over, and the regression line is nearly flat. However, the value of r is not zero (r = 0.136). So, how can we say these two variables aren't correlated? We can say it because the odds are very high that this correlation is nothing but a random accident.

In Exercise 3 you will learn how political scientists calculate the odds as to whether or not a correlation is random. Here it is sufficient to know that many correlations are so small, we treat them *as if they were zero*. And the software automatically does that calculation for you and gives you the results. If you look back at the correlation between income and income tax, you will see that there are two asterisks following the value of r (r = 0.753**). Two asterisks means that there is less than 1 chance in 100 that this correlation is a random accident. One asterisk means that the odds against a correlation being random are 20 to 1. Whenever there are no asterisks following a correlation, the odds are too high that it could be random.[1] That's how we know that the correlation between mobile homes and the Sunbelt is too small to matter—there are no asterisks. *Treat all correlations without asterisks as zero correlations.*

Keep in mind, however, that correlation and causation are not the same thing. It is true that without correlation there can be no causation. But correlations often occur between two variables without one being a cause of the other. And we often are interested in correlations between two variables even when we don't think one causes the other. For example, we might wonder if states having a lot of federal land also have a lot of unattached men—that is, households lacking an adult female resident.

To see if these two variables are correlated, we will go back to the MAPPING function.

Data File: **STATES**
➤ Task: **Mapping**
➤ Variable 1: **17) %FED LAND**
➤ Variable 2: **30) MALE HOMES**
➤ Views: **Map**

%FED LAND -- Percent of State's Area That Is Owned by the Federal Gov't. (SR)

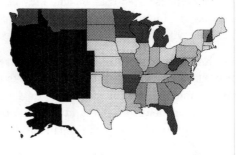

r = 0.628**

MALE HOMES -- Percent of Households without an Adult Female Resident (Census)

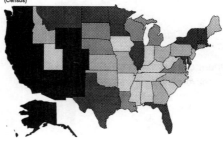

---

[1] As you'll find in the next exercise, statistical significance in survey data helps us to assess whether or not a relationship exists in the population from which the survey sample was drawn. In ecological data sets, such as the 50 states, statistical significance helps us determine whether the existing relationship is a result of chance factors.

The maps do look much alike as both variables are highest in the West. Pearson's r (r = 0.628**) is already calculated for you when two maps are displayed at once. The scatterplot shows how correlations are calculated, but the software does it whenever you compare maps too. The two asterisks show that this is a very strong correlation. But it does not show that one variable is causing the other. An oversupply of all-male households is not the cause of large federal land holdings, and federal land does not prevent marriage. Both variables are simply higher in the West.

Your turn.

EXERCISE 3

"OF THE PEOPLE": AN INTERESTED AND INFORMED PUBLIC

. . . government of the people, by the people, for the people . . .

ABRAHAM LINCOLN,
GETTYSBURG ADDRESS,
NOV. 19, 1863

Tasks: Mapping, Univariate, Cross-Tabulation, Auto-Analyzer
Data Files: NATIONS, NES

While not everyone would agree completely on the details of what we can loosely call democratic theory, there are certain ideas that most democratic theorists would agree on. Most would agree, for example, that a democratic government must be responsive to the will of the people and that it must act in accord with at least some definition of the public good. On the other side of this coin, democratic theory also makes certain assumptions about the citizen. In order for the government to represent the people, citizens must take an interest in public affairs and be adequately informed about them. (Democratic theory also assumes that citizens participate in politics, and we will return to political participation in Exercise 8.) Let's begin with interest in politics.

➤ *Data File:* **NATIONS**
➤ *Task:* **Mapping**
➤ *Variable 1:* **3) P.INTEREST**
➤ *View:* **Map**

P.INTEREST -- Percent Very or Somewhat Interested in Politics (WVS)

This map is based on public opinion polls conducted in 41 nations during 1991. The same questions (translated into the local language) were asked in each poll. Here we see how people responded when asked "How interested would you say you are in politics?"

Data File: **NATIONS**
Task: **Mapping**
Variable 1: **3) P.INTEREST**
➤ View: **List: Rank**

RANK	CASE NAME	VALUE
1	Latvia	79
2	Czech Republic	75
3	Germany	74
4	South Korea	73
4	Bulgaria	73
4	Lithuania	73
7	Norway	72
8	Switzerland	66
9	Japan	62
9	Netherlands	62

People in Latvia were most apt to say that they were "very" or "somewhat" interested in politics, closely followed by the Czechs and the Germans. The Japanese (62 percent) and Chinese (62 percent) were slightly more interested in politics than were Americans, who were tied with Slovaks and Estonians at 59 percent, while 58 percent of Canadians were very or somewhat interested in politics. In contrast, in many nations, including Mexico, Italy, and India, only about a third were interested in politics and in Romania only 18 percent were interested.

Data File: **NATIONS**
Task: **Mapping**
➤ Variable 1: **4) TALK POL.**
➤ View: **Map**

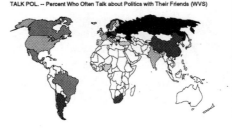

TALK POL. -- Percent Who Often Talk about Politics with Their Friends (WVS)

This map shows variations across nations in the percentage who answered "often" to the question "When you get together with your friends, would you say you discuss political matters frequently, occasionally, or never?"

Data File: **NATIONS**
Task: **Mapping**
Variable 1: **4) TALK POL.**
➤ View: **List: Rank**

RANK	CASE NAME	VALUE
1	Latvia	47
2	Lithuania	45
3	Bulgaria	42
3	Estonia	42
5	Czech Republic	33
5	Belarus	33
5	Germany	33
8	Russia	31
9	Slovak Republic	30
10	Argentina	28

Part I: Foundations

Again, Latvians rank highest, at 47 percent, in talking about politics. Indeed, people in the nations of Eastern Europe, once part of the Soviet bloc, do the most talking about politics. Only 14 percent of Americans frequently talk politics, and only 6 percent of the Japanese do.

➤ *Data File:* **NES**
➤ *Task:* **Univariate**
➤ *Primary Variable:* **3) INTEREST?**
➤ *View:* **Pie**

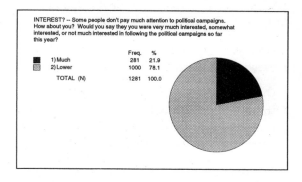

Note that this task uses a new data file.

Here are the results of a national survey of American adults conducted during the 1998 congressional election. This opinion survey, known as the *National Election Study*, is conducted every two years during the national election campaigns by the Institute for Social Research of the University of Michigan. During the interview, each respondent was asked about his or her interest in the political campaigns. Slightly more than one fifth (21.9 percent) of the interviewees indicated a high level of interest; the rest had less interest.

You probably take opinion polling for granted—you have been encountering survey findings in the news media as long as you can remember. Nevertheless, you may have wondered how it is possible to assess the distribution of political opinions among more than 260 million Americans, 150 million Russians, or more than 1 billion Chinese on the basis of interviews conducted with only 1,000 to 2,000 people. The answer is to be found in the **laws of probability**.

Just as a sophisticated gambler can calculate the odds involved in a particular bet, so too political scientists know how to calculate the odds that findings based on a sample of the population yield an accurate portrait of that population. And just as gamblers assume that they are participating in a random game (that the deck has not been stacked or the dice loaded), so too the odds on a sample being accurate depend on the sample being selected at random from the population.

Thus, the first principle of accurate polling is that people are selected by using **random sampling**. For example, interviewers conducting telephone polls often use random dialing software to place their calls. This produces a random sample of all telephones (including those with unlisted numbers) and therefore a random sample of households (except for the 1 percent having no phone). The most careful pollsters then randomly sample a person in each selected household.

If the sample is selected at random, we can use the laws of probability to calculate the odds that what we find accurately reflects the population from which the sample was drawn. These odds are determined by two factors: the size of the sample and the size of observed differences within the sample.

First of all, the sample must be **sufficiently large**. Obviously, we couldn't use a sample of two people as the basis for describing the American population—there is a very high probability that they both would be white. For this reason, survey studies include enough cases so that they can accurately reflect the population in terms of variations in such characteristics as age, sex, education, religion, and the like. The accuracy of a random sample is a function of its size: the larger the sample, the more accurate it is. Oddly enough, accuracy depends only on the size of the sample, not on the size of the sample relative to the size of the population from which the sample is drawn. Thus, a sample of 1,000 persons will yield an equally accurate description of the populations of Fargo, North Dakota, New York City, or the whole United States.

Good survey samples include at least 1,000 persons. The National Election Survey we are using in this exercise is based on 1,281 Americans, and therefore the results are very accurate.

Often, news reports of surveys of public opinion consist of the percentages in favor of or against something—usually something controversial. Unfortunately, too often these "surveys" are not based on randomly selected samples (as when people are invited to register their opinions by dialing an 800 number) or are based on samples that are far too small to be accurate.

The data we have examined thus far report the distribution of opinions of entire populations, for example, how interested are Russians, Canadians, or Americans in politics. However, often we wish *to compare* the opinions of various *groups* within the population. For example, are Americans more or less interested in politics depending on their region?

		Data File:	**NES**
	➤	Task:	**Cross-tabulation**
	➤	Row Variable:	**3) INTEREST?**
➤		Column Variable:	**46) REGION**
	➤	View:	**Table**
	➤	Display:	**Column %**

INTEREST? by REGION
Cramer's V: 0.055

		REGION				
		East	West	Midwest	South	TOTAL
INTEREST?	Much	40	68	69	104	281
		18.9%	25.8%	20.5%	22.2%	21.9%
	Lower	172	196	267	365	1000
		81.1%	74.2%	79.5%	77.8%	78.1%
	TOTAL	212	264	336	469	1281
		100.0%	100.0%	100.0%	100.0%	

To construct this table, return to the main menu and select the CROSS-TABULATION task, then select 3) INTEREST? as the row variable and 46) REGION as the column variable. When the table is showing, select the [Column %] option.

Here, region, as defined by the Bureau of the Census, is divided into four areas. The table reveals that people living in the West (25.8 percent) are more apt than people in other regions to be rated as highly interested in politics. People in the East are least apt to be interested (18.9 percent) with Southerners (22.2 percent) and Midwesterners (20.5 percent) falling in between.

Here, however, we must deal with a second limitation on the accuracy of survey results, one that has to do with the **magnitude of the difference** observed in the table. Simply put, if the difference between the percentaged results is high (e.g., 80% of Westerners are very interested in political campaigns, compared to 30% of Easterners), then the odds that a difference actually exists in the full population are very good. But if the percentaged differences are small (25% of Westerners are very interested in political campaigns, compared to 22% of Easterners), then there is an increased chance that these differences are simply due to randomness, rather than some actual difference in the population. Think about it this way. Suppose you have a bag containing 1,000 marbles. If after drawing out 100 of the marbles you find that 90 are black and 10 are white, you can be pretty confident in stating that there are many more black marbles remaining in the bag than white marbles. However, if you draw out 55 black marbles and 45 white marbles, you will be less confident in stating that there are more black marbles than white marbles remaining in the bag. Thus, in addition to the overall size of the sample, *the size of the difference within the sample* must be considered. The larger the difference that is observed, the greater the probability that it is representative of the population.

These two limits apply because samples are based on the principle of random selection, and therefore they are subject to some degree of *random fluctuation*. That is, for purely random reasons there can be small differences between the sample and the population. Thus, whenever we examine cross-tabulations such as the one shown above, political scientists always must ask whether what they are seeing is a real difference—one that would turn up if the entire population were examined—or only a random fluctuation, which does not reflect a true difference in the population.

The small size of the regional differences observed above (on a sample this size) will always make an experienced analyst suspicious that it is merely the result of random fluctuations. Fortunately, there is a simple technique for calculating the odds that a given difference is real or random. This calculation is called a **test of statistical significance**. Differences observed in samples are said to be statistically significant when the odds against random results are high enough. There is no mathematical way to determine just how high is high enough. But, through the years, social scientists have settled on the rule of thumb that they will ignore all differences (or correlations) unless the odds are at least 20 to 1 against their being random. Put another way, social scientists reject all findings when the probability they are random is greater than .05, or 5 in 100. What this level of significance means is that if 100 random samples were drawn independently from the same population, a difference this large would not turn up more than 5 times, purely by chance.

There are two ways to see what the level of significance is for this table. If you want to know the exact probability of whether the results may be due to random fluctuations, you need to switch to the statistics view.

<table>
<tr><td align="right">Data File:</td><td>**NES**</td></tr>
<tr><td align="right">Task:</td><td>**Cross-tabulation**</td></tr>
<tr><td align="right">Row Variable:</td><td>**3) INTEREST?**</td></tr>
<tr><td align="right">Column Variable:</td><td>**46) REGION**</td></tr>
<tr><td align="right">View:</td><td>**Table**</td></tr>
<tr><td align="right">➤ Display:</td><td>**Statistics (Summary)**</td></tr>
</table>

INTEREST?   by   REGION

Nominal Statistics

Chi-Square: 3.817	(DF =	3; Prob. = 0.282)			
V:	0.055	C:	0.055		
Lambda: (DV=46)	0.000	Lambda: (DV=3)	0.000	Lambda:	0.000

Ordinal Statistics

Gamma:	-0.009	Tau-b:	-0.005	Tau-c:	-0.005
s.error	0.051	s.error	0.025	s.error	0.025
Dyx	-0.003	Dxy:	-0.007		
s.error	0.017	s.error	0.037		
Prob. =	0.859				

Ignore everything on this screen except for the first two lines of text. At the end of the first line you'll see "Prob. = 0.282." This value indicates that the odds these results are simply due to randomness are 282 in 1,000 (or about 3 in 10). Since social scientists require that these odds be less than 1 in 20 (.05), we know that the slight regional differences between those who were highly interested in the campaign might be due to random fluctuations.

There is another number on this screen that you'll find useful when doing cross-tabulation analysis. In the second row, locate the value "V = 0.055." The V stands for Cramer's V, which is a correlation coefficient developed for cross-tabulations. Cramer's V is similar to Pearson's r (see Exercise 2) in that its value varies from 0 to 1. If the relationship between these two variables was perfect (that is, if all people in the West indicated they were very interested in the political campaign while all people in the East indicated they were not interested in the political campaign), then this would be a value of 1.

However, unlike Pearson's r, V does not indicate whether the relationship is positive or negative—the kind of relationship must be inferred from the table itself. Also, it should be noted that survey data produce much lower correlations than do data based on aggregates such as states or nations. For our purposes, let's use the following guidelines to assess the strength of Cramer's V.

- If V is between .00 and .10, the relationship is very weak or nonexistent.

- If V is between .10 and .25, the relationship is moderate.

- If V is over .25, the relationship is strong.

For this table, V is only .055. Thus, there is virtually no strength to this relationship and it is not important.

It's important to understand that Cramer's V assesses the strength of the relationship shown in the table, not the odds that the results are statistically significant. Don't confuse Cramer's V with the probability value—they provide different information.

Here's something else to remember. Sometimes in large surveys like the GSS, you'll see differences in tables of only 2 to 3 percentage points, yet they are statistically significant. Even if this difference does exist in the entire population, it's generally not worthy of note. Whenever you examine cross-tabulations in this book, always look at the actual difference in percentage points. If the difference is less than 5 or 10 percentage points, ask yourself whether it's substantively significant.

Hence, when doing cross-tabulation analysis, you should follow these steps. First, look at the table to see if the observed differences are worth noting. If the categories you are comparing differ by fewer than 5 to 10 percentage points, the analysis may not be worth pursuing. Second, if you are testing a hypothesis, be sure that the percentages differ in the predicted direction. For instance, if you predict that men are more likely than women to be interested in politics, then the differences in the table should support this. Assuming you make it through the first two steps, the third step is to look at the actual strength of the relationship by examining the correlation coefficient (V). Finally, determine whether the results are statistically significant. It's in this final step that you apply the .05 rule described earlier.

The CROSS-TABULATION task in ExplorIt makes this process even easier by placing all the information needed on one screen. Return to the [Column %] option to view the table again. Notice that the value of V appears at the top of this screen too. If these results were statistically significant at the .05 level, one asterisk would appear after this value. If these results were significant at the .01 level (making the odds 1 in 100), two asterisks would appear. Since there are no asterisks following the V value, we know that these regional differences are too small to be statistically significant.

The following chart sums up the process of "Assessing a Relationship Between Variables in a Cross-Tabulation." If you need guidelines, just follow the steps in this chart.

ASSESSING A RELATIONSHIP BETWEEN VARIABLES IN A CROSS-TABULATION

Step 1:   Determine whether the observed differences are worth noting. Example: Are the differences in political interest between men and women big enough to be important?

↓   ↓

The differences are only a few percentage points.   The differences are at least 5–10 percentage points.

↓   ↓

The relationship is not important.   The relationship might be important.

↓

Step 2:   If testing a hypothesis, check whether the results are in the hypothesized direction. For example, if you hypothesized that men would have higher political interest than women, are the results in accord with this?

↓

Step 3:   Examine the strength of the relationship by looking at the correlation coefficient, Cramer's V.

↓

Step 4:   Determine whether the results are statistically significant.

↓   ↓

The significance level is .05 or less —there is at least one asterisk next to Cramer's V.   The significance level is greater than .05—there is no asterisk next to Cramer's V.

↓   ↓

The relationship is statistically significant. We decide that there is a real relationship between the variables in the population from which the sample was selected.   The relationship is not statistically significant. We decide that there is no real relationship between the variables in the population.

Let's examine another example.

<table>
<tr><td>Data File:</td><td>NES</td></tr>
<tr><td>Task:</td><td>Cross-tabulation</td></tr>
<tr><td>Row Variable:</td><td>3) INTEREST?</td></tr>
<tr><td>➤ Column Variable:</td><td>47) AGE</td></tr>
<tr><td>➤ View:</td><td>Table</td></tr>
<tr><td>➤ Display:</td><td>Column %</td></tr>
</table>

INTEREST? by AGE
Cramer's V: 0.221 **

		AGE						
		Under 30	30 to 39	40 to 49	50 to 64	65 & Over	Missing	TOTAL
INTEREST?	Much	23	39	72	68	76	3	278
		9.5%	14.3%	25.9%	25.7%	36.5%		22.0%
	Lower	219	233	206	197	132	13	987
		90.5%	85.7%	74.1%	74.3%	63.5%		78.0%
	TOTAL	242	272	278	265	208	16	1265
		100.0%	100.0%	100.0%	100.0%	100.0%		

Reading and comparing across the values for the first *row*, we discover that older people are more interested in politics than are younger people. Cramer's V is 0.221, which is moderately strong. The two asterisks indicate that the odds are less than 1 in 100 that these age differences are random. We can have a lot of confidence that in this instance age really matters.

Does one's education level affect the level of interest he or she has in politics?

<table>
<tr><td>Data File:</td><td>NES</td></tr>
<tr><td>Task:</td><td>Cross-tabulation</td></tr>
<tr><td>Row Variable:</td><td>3) INTEREST?</td></tr>
<tr><td>➤ Column Variable:</td><td>48) EDUCATION</td></tr>
<tr><td>➤ View:</td><td>Table</td></tr>
<tr><td>➤ Display:</td><td>Column %</td></tr>
</table>

INTEREST? by EDUCATION
Cramer's V: 0.172 **

		EDUCATION					
		Not HS Grd	HS Grad	Some Col	Coll.Grad.	Missing	TOTAL
INTEREST?	Much	30	51	88	111	1	280
		17.8%	13.2%	24.0%	31.3%		21.9%
	Lower	139	335	278	244	4	996
		82.2%	86.8%	76.0%	68.7%		78.1%
	TOTAL	169	386	366	355	5	1276
		100.0%	100.0%	100.0%	100.0%		

We easily can see in the table that more educated people are more likely to be interested in politics. Once again the relationship is fairly strong (V = 0.172) and the results are statistically significant at the .01 level, as indicated by the two asterisks. Let's examine another key demographic: gender.

<table>
<tr><td>Data File:</td><td>NES</td></tr>
<tr><td>Task:</td><td>Cross-tabulation</td></tr>
<tr><td>Row Variable:</td><td>3) INTEREST?</td></tr>
<tr><td>➤ Column Variable:</td><td>41) SEX</td></tr>
<tr><td>➤ View:</td><td>Table</td></tr>
<tr><td>➤ Display:</td><td>Column %</td></tr>
</table>

INTEREST? by SEX
Cramer's V: 0.045

		SEX		
		Male	Female	TOTAL
INTEREST?	Much	138	143	281
		24.0%	20.3%	21.9%
	Lower	437	563	1000
		76.0%	79.7%	78.1%
	TOTAL	575	706	1281
		100.0%	100.0%	

The table shows that men (24.0 percent) are more apt to be interested in political campaigns than are women (20.3 percent). Notice, however, there is less than a 4 percentage point difference between men and women. This small difference does not have much substantive significance—even if the results are statistically significant. In this situation, both men and women lack interest in politics and the difference between them is so small that it is not important. In this particular example, the summary statistics reiterate the weak relationship: Cramer's V is very slight (0.045), and the results are not statistically significant.

When political scientists study a particular behavior or attitude, they first examine the overall distribution (such as a pie chart) of that attitude. For example, one of the first things we looked at in this exercise was the percentage of Americans who indicate they are very interested in the campaign, what percentage have some interest, and so on. Next, political scientists look at the relationship between that variable and various demographic variables, such as age, education, gender, and so on. We did the same thing in this exercise using the technique of cross-tabulation to see how interest in politics is distributed in the population. This type of preliminary analysis provides a snapshot of the population with regard to the variable of interest.

For the next two examples, let's use the AUTO-ANALYZER task that is available on the main menu.

Data File:	**NES**			
➤ Task:	**Auto-Analyzer**			
➤ Variable:	**3) INTEREST?**			
➤ View:	**Univariate**			

	PERCENT
Much	21.9%
Lower	78.1%

Among all respondents, 21.9% of the sample had expressed much interest in the political campaigns.

To obtain these results, return to the main menu and select the AUTO-ANALYZER task. Then select 3) INTEREST? as your analyzer variable and click [OK].

The first result that Auto-Analyzer provides is the *univariate* distribution for the variable you selected. As you can see, the percentages are the same as what we found earlier using the UNIVARIATE task from the main menu. As the textual summary indicates, among all respondents, 21.9 percent of the sample had expressed much interest in the political campaigns.

Data File:	**NES**
Task:	**Auto-Analyzer**
Variable:	**3) INTEREST?**
➤ View:	**Race**

	RACE	
	White	African American
Much	20.8%	30.3%
Lower	79.2%	69.7%

Among African Americans, 30.3% had expressed much interest in the political campaigns. Among whites, this percentage was only 20.8%. The difference is statistically significant.

If continuing from the previous example, simply click the button [Race] to see the results.

These results are identical to what you would obtain if you cross-tabulated the variable INTEREST? with RACE. The only difference is that it is not necessary for you to percentage the table and a summary of the table is provided. As shown by the description, African Americans were more interested in the political campaign than were white Americans. As noted, the differences are statistically significant.[1]

---

[1] In some cases, the significance of V on the table and the significance given in Auto-Analyzer may be slightly different. The statistic V is used in the CROSS-TABULATION task and is based on chi-square, which summarizes the entire table. Auto-Analyzer relies on column-by-column comparisons in an attempt to uncover patterns of interest. In other words, these two tasks focus on slightly different aspects of the results.

In the worksheets, you'll have a chance to explore several attitudes using the AUTO-ANALYZER task. You will also find this task useful in doing exploratory analysis for papers or projects you may work on for this and other classes.

Your turn.

Part II

FREEDOM: CIVIL LIBERTIES AND CIVIL RIGHTS

Exercise 4   **Civil Liberties: Free Speech**

Exercise 5   **Civil Rights: Equality**

When people speak of the United States as a "free country," they have two basic kinds of freedom in mind. The first kind of freedom consists of what are called **civil liberties**. These include freedom of speech, press, religion, assembly, and petition. The Bill of Rights guarantees these freedoms from infringement by the government or by citizen-groups. If a mob shouts down a speaker, they are denying his or her civil liberties. If the government forbids an unpopular group from expressing their views, that too is a violation of their civil liberties.

The second kind of freedom consists of **civil rights**. These include all the rights of democratic citizenship including voting, equal treatment before the law, an equal share of public benefits, and equal access to public facilities. When African Americans were excluded from voting and from jury duty, and denied access to park benches in the South, they were being denied their civil rights.

In the next two exercises, you will examine public opinion about civil liberties and civil rights.

EXERCISE **4**

CIVIL LIBERTIES: FREE SPEECH

Congress shall make no law respecting an establishment of religion, or prohibiting free exercise thereof; of abridging the freedom of speech, or of the press; or the right of the people peaceably to assemble, and to petition the government for a redress of grievances.

FIRST AMENDMENT TO
THE CONSTITUTION,
RATIFIED IN 1791

Tasks: Mapping, Univariate, Cross-Tabulation, Scatterplot, Historical Trends, Auto-Analyzer
Data Files: NATIONS, GSS, HISTORY

The Bill of Rights was written and adopted because there was widespread public concern that, because these civil liberties were not specifically guaranteed by the Constitution, future governments might fail to uphold them. Many amendments making up the Bill of Rights are concerned with keeping the government from committing abuses such as failing to hold a speedy trial or forcing people to testify against themselves in court. But the five freedoms mentioned in the First Amendment (shown above) concern freedom of expression. The first-mentioned freedom in the First Amendment concerns an establishment of religion and the free exercise of religion. Sometimes the religious freedom clauses (known as the establishment clause and the free exercise clause) in the First Amendment are referred to as the "First Freedom" because they were listed first. James Madison, the "Father of the Constitution," was certainly very concerned with religious freedom. He and Jefferson had fought a series of battles in Virginia to protect religious liberty and to prevent the state from favoring one religion over another. Throughout history, many of the battles concerning freedom of expression have been fought over issues of religious liberty.

The other four freedoms in the First Amendment are concerned primarily with enabling people to influence and change the government. The Constitution itself provides the means by which it can be amended. But, without the freedom to speak, write, assemble, or petition, the people would lack the political means to amend the Constitution, influence officials, affect public policy, or successfully vote "the rascals" out of office. Of course, the rights of free speech and a free press extend far beyond direct applications to politics, but these remain the most basic aspects of freedom.

> *Data File:* **NATIONS**
> *Task:* **Mapping**
> *Variable 1:* **6) PETITION?**
> *View:* **Map**

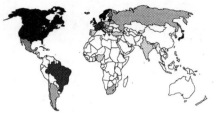

PETITION? -- Percent Who Have Signed a Political Petition (WVS)

This map shows how people in many nations responded when asked whether they had ever signed a political petition.

Data File: **NATIONS**
Task: **Mapping**
Variable 1: **6) PETITION?**
> *View:* **List: Rank**

RANK	CASE NAME	VALUE
1	Canada	77
2	Great Britain	75
3	Sweden	72
4	United States	71
5	Latvia	65
6	Switzerland	63
7	Japan	62
8	Norway	61
9	Germany	60
10	Lithuania	58

More than 7 out of 10 people in Canada, Great Britain, Sweden, and the United States have used their freedom to petition their government. But in many countries few have signed petitions: 14 percent in Turkey and Poland and only 5 percent in Nigeria. Keep in mind that nations with high levels of political freedom are very overrepresented among these nations—public opinion polling is itself an aspect of political expression and therefore is discouraged or controlled in some nations (which is one reason this question was not asked in the Chinese survey).

Regardless of what constitutions say about civil liberties, however, a major factor always is the extent to which the citizens are committed to maintaining these rights. Thus, for example, if enough Americans became disgusted with free speech, they would have the right to repeal the First Amendment and substitute laws limiting free speech. Moreover, in actual practice the extent to which people do have free speech depends to some extent on the degree to which other Americans respect that right. "Freedom of speech" is not really a freedom unless people feel free to use it. If a person holds unpopular opinions, other people might resist allowing that person to present his or her views—or they might retaliate against the person for presenting unpopular views. So, let's explore public commitment to free speech.

Part II: Freedom: Civil Liberties and Civil Rights

> *Data File:* **GSS**
> *Task:* **Univariate**
> *Primary Variable:* **23) ATHEIST SP**
> *View:* **Pie**

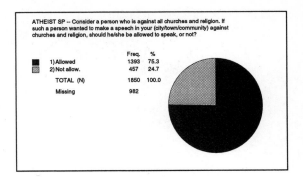

The 1998 General Social Surveys asks: "Consider a person who is against all churches and religion. If such a person wanted to make a speech in your (city/town/community) against churches and religion, should he/she be allowed to speak, or not?"

Here we see that 75 percent of those polled would allow an atheist to make a speech. The GSS has been asking Americans this question since 1972, when about 67 percent said the speech should be allowed. But the history of this question goes back to a famous survey by Samuel Stouffer in 1954 during the "McCarthy era" when only 37 percent would allow the speech.[1]

Let's see if this attitude toward freedom of speech is the same in all regions.

Data File: **GSS**
> *Task:* **Cross-tabulation**
> *Row Variable:* **23) ATHEIST SP**
> *Column Variable:* **65) REGION**
> *View:* **Table**
> *Display:* **Column %**

ATHEIST SP   by   REGION
Cramer's V: 0.125 **

		REGION				
		East	Midwest	South	West	TOTAL
ATHEIST SP	Allowed	292	335	457	309	1393
		78.9%	74.3%	69.3%	83.5%	75.3%
	Not allow.	78	116	202	61	457
		21.1%	25.7%	30.7%	16.5%	24.7%
	Missing	199	245	362	176	982
	TOTAL	370	451	659	370	1850
		100.0%	100.0%	100.0%	100.0%	

Westerners are most likely (83.5 percent) to allow an atheist to speak, and Southerners are least likely (69.3 percent). The difference is statistically significant (V = 0.125**). Perhaps this regional difference is more about dislike of atheists than about general attitudes about freedom of speech. One way to find out is to see if the regional differences persist on a different aspect of free speech. What about freedom to give racist speeches?

---

[1] Samuel Stouffer, *Communism, Conformity, and Civil Liberties* (New York: Doubleday, 1955).

Data File: **GSS**
➤ Task: **Univariate**
➤ Primary Variable: **25) RACIST SP**
➤ View: **Pie**

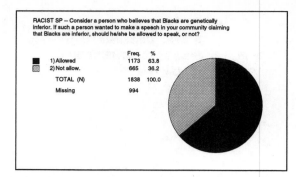

Overall, Americans are less willing to give free speech to "a person who believes that Blacks are genetically inferior," but here too the majority is in favor of allowing the person to speak.

Data File: **GSS**
➤ Task: **Cross-tabulation**
➤ Row Variable: **25) RACIST SP**
➤ Column Variable: **65) REGION**
➤ View: **Table**
➤ Display: **Column %**

RACIST SP   by   REGION
Cramer's V: 0.048

		REGION				
		East	Midwest	South	West	TOTAL
RACIST SP	Allowed	240	291	396	246	1173
		64.5%	64.8%	60.9%	67.0%	63.8%
	Not allow.	132	158	254	121	665
		35.5%	35.2%	39.1%	33.0%	36.2%
	Missing	197	247	371	179	994
	TOTAL	372	449	650	367	1838
		100.0%	100.0%	100.0%	100.0%	

And once again Westerners are most likely (67.0 percent) to support free speech and Southerners are least likely (60.9 percent). However, the difference is not statistically significant (V = 0.048).

Let's look at a third test of support for free speech.

Data File: **GSS**
➤ Task: **Univariate**
➤ Primary Variable: **24) COMMUN.SP**
➤ View: **Pie**

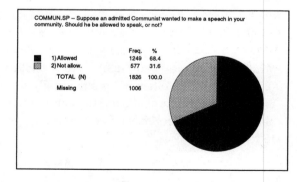

Overall, Americans are a bit more willing to give free speech to "an admitted Communist" than to a racist.

Data File: **GSS**
➤ *Task:* **Cross-tabulation**
➤ *Row Variable:* **24) COMMUN.SP**
➤ *Column Variable:* **65) REGION**
➤ *View:* **Table**
➤ *Display:* **Column %**

COMMUN.SP by REGION
Cramer's V: 0.137 **

		REGION				
		East	Midwest	South	West	TOTAL
COMMUN.SP	Allowed	260	303	397	289	1249
		69.7%	67.6%	61.8%	79.6%	68.4%
	Not allow.	113	145	245	74	577
		30.3%	32.4%	38.2%	20.4%	31.6%
	Missing	196	248	379	183	1006
	TOTAL	373	448	642	363	1826
		100.0%	100.0%	100.0%	100.0%	

And, for the third time, Southerners are least likely to support free speech. Since V = 0.137**, the difference is statistically significant.

The consistency of these findings reflects the fact that each of these three questions really measures the same thing: support for free speech. When political scientists use multiple measures of something, they often combine the results into a single measure called an attitude index or scale.

An **attitude index** measures an attitude on the basis of answers to several questions believed to be measures of the same general attitude. The logic involved is the same logic teachers use when they construct an examination. For example, when teachers give a test made up of true/false or multiple-choice questions, they don't just ask one or two questions. They ask many. They do so because they know that even the best-prepared students can miss any given question and that the worst students could get any particular answer right. So, teachers give tests asking a lot of questions in order to get a more accurate measure of what students have learned.

Just as individual scores on a test are calculated on the basis of the number of correct (or incorrect) answers, attitude indexes "add up" values assigned to some set of questions. In this instance we have three questions measuring support for free speech. Suppose we give each respondent a point for every question to which he or she answered "not allowed" and no points for "allowed" answers. Thus, people who would extend freedom of speech in all three instances would score 0 and those who would deny free speech in all three instances would score 3. To simplify the index slightly, we will combine people with scores of 1 and 2 to make a single category (moderate support for free speech) so that there will be only three rather than four categories.

Data File: **GSS**
➤ *Task:* **Univariate**
➤ *Primary Variable:* **26) FR.SPEECH**
➤ *View:* **Pie**

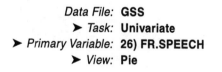

FR.SPEECH -- Score on Index of Support for Freedom of Speech

		Freq.	%
■	1) High	962	54.0
▨	2) Medium	536	30.1
■	3) Low	283	15.9
	TOTAL (N)	1781	100.0
	Missing	1051	

All things considered, Americans have considerable respect for freedom of speech—more than half (54.0 percent) would extend free speech in all three instances. On the other hand, these results suggest that almost half of the American citizenry would deny freedom of speech to some people. Let's examine the results by region again.

Data File: **GSS**
➤ Task: **Cross-tabulation**
➤ Row Variable: **26) FR.SPEECH**
➤ Column Variable: **65) REGION**
➤ View: **Table**
➤ Display: **Column %**

FR.SPEECH   by   REGION
Cramer's V: 0.109 **

		REGION				
		East	Midwest	South	West	TOTAL
FR.SPEECH	High	190	240	312	220	962
		52.9%	54.7%	49.9%	61.5%	54.0%
	Medium	133	121	179	103	536
		37.0%	27.6%	28.6%	28.8%	30.1%
	Low	36	78	134	35	283
		10.0%	17.8%	21.4%	9.8%	15.9%
	Missing	210	257	396	188	1051
	TOTAL	359	439	625	358	1781
		100.0%	100.0%	100.0%	100.0%	

Not surprisingly, support for free speech is highest in the West and lowest in the South.

➤ Data File: **NATIONS**
➤ Task: **Mapping**
➤ Variable 1: **19) CIVIL LIBS**
➤ View: **Map**

CIVIL LIBS -- Index of Civil Liberties, Higher = Greater Liberty (FITW, 1997)

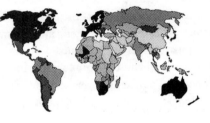

Using the same logic as used to construct the index of support for free speech, each year an American organization known as Freedom House scores every nation (including the tiny ones) on an index of civil liberties. Those nations that sustain the maximum amount of civil liberties are scored 7, and the scores go as low as 1 for nations in which people do not have civil liberties.

Data File: **NATIONS**
Task: **Mapping**
Variable 1: **19) CIVIL LIBS**
➤ View: **List: Rank**

RANK	CASE NAME	VALUE
1	Finland	7
1	Luxembourg	7
1	Canada	7
1	Malta	7
1	Belize	7
1	Barbados	7
1	Denmark	7
1	Ireland	7
1	Portugal	7
1	Switzerland	7

Here we see that a number of nations including the United States and Canada were scored 7 in civil liberties. At the bottom of the ranking, we find that 18 countries were scored 1.

<table>
<tr><td align="right">Data File:</td><td>NATIONS</td></tr>
<tr><td align="right">Task:</td><td>Mapping</td></tr>
<tr><td align="right">Variable 1:</td><td>19) CIVIL LIBS</td></tr>
<tr><td align="right">➤ Variable 2:</td><td>6) PETITION?</td></tr>
<tr><td align="right">➤ Views:</td><td>Map</td></tr>
</table>

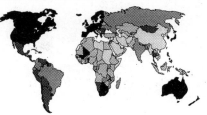

CIVIL LIBS -- Index of Civil Liberties, Higher = Greater Liberty (FITW, 1997)

r = 0.569**

PETITION? -- Percent Who Have Signed a Political Petition (WVS)

As would be expected, there is a very high correlation (r = 0.569**) between scores on the civil liberties index and the percentage in each nation who said they had signed a petition.

Sometimes it is argued that allowing freedom of expression to the people of a country allows them to express their frustrations and that this will prevent pressure from building up that might lead to rebellion. Let's cross-tabulate the civil liberties index by the percentage in nations that agreed their society must be changed radically by revolutionary action.

<table>
<tr><td align="right">Data File:</td><td>NATIONS</td></tr>
<tr><td align="right">Task:</td><td>Mapping</td></tr>
<tr><td align="right">Variable 1:</td><td>19) CIVIL LIBS</td></tr>
<tr><td align="right">➤ Variable 2:</td><td>9) REVOLUTION</td></tr>
<tr><td align="right">➤ Views:</td><td>Map</td></tr>
</table>

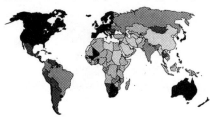

CIVIL LIBS -- Index of Civil Liberties, Higher = Greater Liberty (FITW, 1997)

r = −0.392**

REVOLUTION -- Percent Who Agree That Their Society Must Be Changed Radically "By Revolutionary Action" (WVS)

We see that there is a statistically significant negative relationship ($r = -0.392$**) between civil liberties in nations and the extent to which people in those nations say that a revolution is needed. This supports the idea that having civil liberties reduces pressures for a rebellion.

Your turn.

WORKSHEET

NAME:

COURSE:

DATE:

EXERCISE

4

REVIEW QUESTIONS

Based on the first part of this exercise, answer True or False to the following items:

Civil rights include such things as the right to assemble and to petition the government.	T F
Most Americans would deny free speech to an atheist.	T F
The West is the region with the greatest support for free speech.	T F
Support for civil liberties is higher in Canada than in the United States.	T F
Freedom of speech is one of the first things guaranteed in the Constitution.	T F
One freedom denied to Americans by their Constitution is the freedom to eliminate civil liberties.	T F
The South is the region with the lowest support for free speech.	T F
The basic freedom of expression rights are contained in the First Amendment to the U.S. Constitution.	T F
People in nations that have more civil liberties are more likely to think that a revolution is needed in their nation.	T F

EXPLORIT QUESTIONS

1. We've found that nations differ in the extent to which civil liberties are supported. Let's see which characteristics of nations may have an effect on this variable. Perhaps the level of democracy?

    > *Data File:* **NATIONS**
    > *Task:* **Mapping**
    > *Variable 1:* **19) CIVIL LIBS**
    > *Variable 2:* **18) DEMOCRACY**
    > *Views:* **Map**

    What is the value of r for these comparison maps?   r = _____

    Is it statistically significant?   Yes   No

Exercise 4: Civil Liberties: Free Speech   73

Which statement best summarizes the relationship between these variables? (Circle the letter of the most appropriate answer.)

    a.   The more democratic the country, the better its civil liberties rating.

    b.   The less democratic the country, the better its civil liberties rating.

    c.   Democracy and civil liberties appear to be unrelated.

2.   Let's examine the effect of education on support of civil liberties. In the NATIONS data file, we will use the estimated education level that citizens of a country are expected to achieve as a measure of education.

                     Data File: **NATIONS**
                ➤ *Task:* **Scatterplot**
    ➤ *Dependent Variable:* **19) CIVIL LIBS**
  ➤ *Independent Variable:* **40) EDUC EXPTD**
                 ➤ *View:* **Reg. Line**

                                               $r =$ _____   Significant? Yes No

Answer True or False to the following items:

There is no relationship between the education level of the populace and the rating on civil liberties.	T	F
Countries with higher education levels tend to score higher on the civil liberties index.	T	F
These results suggest that there may be a causal relationship between education and civil liberties.	T	F

3.   Let's look at educational level and attitude toward free speech over time in the United States.

         ➤ *Data File:* **HISTORY**
            ➤ *Task:* **Historical Trends**
        ➤ *Variables:* **28) CIVLIB INX**
                     7) %COLLEGE

Open the HISTORY data file and select the HISTORICAL TRENDS task. Select 28) CIVLIB INX and 7) %COLLEGE as your trend variables.

Because the GSS was not started until the 1970s, comparable data in the index are not available prior to 1970.

What is the description of 28) CIVLIB INX? _____

_____

_____

What is the description of 7) %COLLEGE?

_____

_____

Over the past 20 years, the percentage opposing free speech has increased
dramatically in the United States.   T   F

The percentage of the population who have graduated from college and the
tolerance for free speech have both increased over the past two decades.   T   F

This graph suggests that an individual's education might affect his or her attitude
toward free speech.   T   F

4.   We can also look at the effect of education on support of free speech using survey data.

> *Data File:*   **GSS**
> *Task:*   **Cross-tabulation**
> *Row Variable:*   **26) FR.SPEECH**
> *Column Variable:* **67) EDUCATION**
> *View:*   **Table**
> *Display:*   **Column %**

Copy the first row of the percentaged table.

	NOT HS GRD	HS GRD	SOME COLL.	COLL GRAD
% SCORING HIGH	_____%	_____%	_____%	_____%

What is the value of V for this table?   V = _____

Is V statistically significant?   Yes   No

The higher one's educational attainment, the less likely one is to endorse
the right of free speech.   T   F

Each additional level of education seems to increase tolerance of free speech.   T   F

5.   Let's see what other characteristics may affect support for free speech.

   Data File: **GSS**
> *Task:*   **Auto-Analyzer**
> *Variable:*   **26) FR.SPEECH**
> *View:*   **Age**

   **First select the AUTO-ANALYZER task and select 26) FR.SPEECH as the analyzer variable.
   Then select the option corresponding to age.**

Carefully review the results for this analysis and then answer True or False to the following items:

About 60 percent of those under age 30 scored high on freedom of speech.   T   F

The age group of 65 and over has the highest percentage who score high on freedom of speech.   T   F

Among those younger than 50, the three age categories are fairly similar in their support for freedom of speech.   T   F

Among those older than 39, the percent high on freedom of speech decreases with age.   T   F

6. Continue to use the AUTO-ANALYZER task and 26) FR.SPEECH to look at the effects of sex, political party, and religion on support of free speech. Carefully look at the tables and summaries for each item. Based on these results and the results of Question 5, describe the person most likely to endorse the right of free speech.

7. Frequently one person's freedom of speech interferes with another person's perceived rights. For example, does the right to freedom of speech include the right to use racial slurs, the right to call for the radical overthrow of the government, and the right to distribute pornography?

> Data File: **GSS**
> ➤ Task: **Univariate**
> ➤ Primary Variable: **43) PORN.LAW?**
> ➤ View: **Pie**

What percentage responded that

1. there should be laws against the distribution of pornography, whatever the age?   _____%

2. there should be laws against the distribution of pornography to persons under age 18?   _____%

3. there should be no laws forbidding the distribution of pornography?   _____%

8. Let's see how a person's attitude toward free speech affects his or her attitude toward the distribution of pornography.

> *Data File:* **GSS**
> ➤ *Task:* **Cross-tabulation**
> ➤ *Row Variable:* **43) PORN.LAW?**
> ➤ *Column Variable:* **26) FR.SPEECH**
> ➤ *View:* **Table**
> ➤ *Display:* **Column %**

Fill in the percentages for the first row of this cross-tabulation—the percentages of persons who would outlaw all pornography.

	HIGH	**MEDIUM**	**LOW**
%YES:ALL	_____%	_____%	_____%

What is the value of Cramer's V for this table?   V = _____

Is V statistically significant?   Yes   No

Which of the following statements most accurately summarizes the relationship between support for freedom of speech and support for outlawing all pornography? (Circle the letter of the most appropriate answer.)

   a. Those who support freedom of speech do not support outlawing pornography.

   b. Those who support freedom of speech also support outlawing pornography.

   c. There is no relationship between support for freedom of speech and support for outlawing pornography.

9. Prior to the 1970s, public schools typically began the day with Bible readings and a prayer. In the 1970s, these school-sponsored religious activities were ruled to be unconstitutional by the Supreme Court. Today, the issue of school prayer is argued as a freedom of expression issue by both those who oppose it and those who favor it. How do attitudes on this issue relate to support for freedom of speech?

> *Data File:* **GSS**
> *Task:* **Cross-tabulation**
> ➤ *Row Variable:* **7) SCH.PRAYER**
> ➤ *Column Variable:* **26) FR.SPEECH**
> ➤ *View:* **Table**
> ➤ *Display:* **Column %**

Fill in the percentages for the first row of this cross-tabulation—the percentages of persons who do not favor school prayer.

	HIGH	**MEDIUM**	**LOW**
% NO PRAYER	_____%	_____%	_____%

What is the value of Cramer's V for this table?   V = _____

Is V statistically significant?   Yes   No

Which of the following statements most accurately summarizes the relationship between support for school prayer and support for freedom of speech? (Circle the letter of the most appropriate answer.)

   a.   Those who support freedom of speech do not support school prayer.

   b.   Those who support freedom of speech also support school prayer.

   c.   There is no relationship between support for freedom of speech and support for school prayer.

10. It has been apparent throughout this analysis that some Americans support freedom of speech more than others. But are those who support freedom of speech in particular situations simply supporting it because they tend to agree with the views of the particular group/person being discussed? To take a particular example, are those who would allow a speech by a racist simply more likely to be racists themselves? Let's test this idea using the question of whether interracial marriage should be outlawed as a measure of whether one holds racist ideas or not.

Data File:	**GSS**
Task:	**Cross-tabulation**
➤ *Row Variable:*	**25 RACIST SP**
➤ *Column Variable:*	**92) INTERMAR.?**
➤ *View:*	**Table**
➤ *Display:*	**Column %**

Fill in the percentages for the first row of this cross-tabulation—the percentages of persons who would allow a speech by a racist.

	YES	NO
% ALLOW	_____%	_____%

What is the value of Cramer's V for this table?   V = _____

Is V statistically significant?   Yes   No

Which of the following statements most accurately summarizes the relationship between willingness to allow a speech by a racist and opposition to laws against interracial marriage? (Circle the letter of the most appropriate answer.)

   a.   Those who took the racist position (the YES position—favor laws against interracial marriage) are more likely to allow a speech by a racist.

   b.   Those who took the nonracist position (the NO position—oppose laws against interracial marriage) are more likely to allow a speech by a racist.

   c.   There is no relationship between willingness to allow a speech by a racist and opposition to laws against interracial marriage.

CIVIL RIGHTS: EQUALITY

We hold these truths to be self-evident: That all men are created equal; that they are endowed by their Creator with certain unalienable rights; that among these are life, liberty, and the pursuit of happiness. . . .

THE DECLARATION OF
INDEPENDENCE,
JULY 4, 1776

Tasks: Mapping, Univariate, Cross-Tabulation, Historical Trends, Scatterplot, Auto-Analyzer
Data Files: NATIONS, GSS, STATES, HISTORY, NES

These shining phrases announced the intention of the American colonists to cast off British rule and assert their "unalienable rights." Unfortunately, as the authors frankly stated, equality did not entirely apply to women ("all men"), and, as they failed to mention, these rights applied not at all to the hundreds of thousands of slaves—many slave-owners were among those who signed the Declaration. Nor did they apply to those inhabitants of America who already were here when Europeans arrived to "discover" the New World.

The struggle to include "all" within the boundaries of equality has gone on since the founding of the nation, and, although civil rights are far more extensive and secure than they were even a few years ago, the politics of "inclusion" and "exclusion" remain a central feature of our time. At a literalist level, one might have thought that the matter of equality would have been solved by the Fourteenth Amendment which, among other things, defines citizenship (all persons born or naturalized in the United States, and subject to the jurisdiction thereof) and prohibits the states from denying any citizen within their jurisdiction the equal protection of the laws. This, of course, was not sufficient. For example, it took the Nineteenth Amendment to give women even the right to vote. The quest for equality has resulted in a variety of civil rights movements as African Americans, women, ethnic and racial minorities, sexual minorities, and others have sought equal treatment.

Nevertheless, Americans too often mistakenly regard our conflicts over civil rights as unique. In fact, conflicts based on racial, ethnic, and cultural prejudices probably are as old as the human race and exist to some degree in all societies.

➤ *Data File:* **NATIONS**
   ➤ *Task:* **Mapping**
➤ *Variable 1:* **11) ANTI-RACE**
   ➤ *View:* **Map**

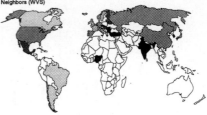

ANTI-RACE -- Percent Who Would Not Want Members of Another Race As Neighbors (WVS)

Here we see the percentage of people in each of 41 nations who indicated that they would not want to have "people of a different race as neighbors."

Data File: **NATIONS**
   Task: **Mapping**
Variable 1: **11) ANTI-RACE**
   ➤ *View:* **List: Rank**

RANK	CASE NAME	VALUE
1	South Korea	58
2	India	44
3	Slovenia	40
4	Bulgaria	39
5	Turkey	34
5	Nigeria	34
5	Slovak Republic	34
8	Czech Republic	28
8	Romania	28
10	Finland	25

The majority of South Koreans don't want people of a different race as neighbors, nor would 44 percent of the populace in India and 40 percent in Slovenia. In contrast, only 10 percent of Americans feel this way and only 5 percent of Canadians.

Data File: **NATIONS**
   Task: **Mapping**
Variable 1: **11) ANTI-RACE**
➤ *Variable 2:* **12) ANTI-FORGN**
   ➤ *Views:* **List: Rank**

RANK	CASE NAME	VALUE
1	South Korea	58
2	India	44
3	Slovenia	40
4	Bulgaria	39
5	Nigeria	34

RANK	CASE NAME	VALUE
1	South Korea	53
2	India	48
3	Slovenia	40
4	Czech Republic	34
4	Bulgaria	34

Select the [List: Rank] option on both the upper and lower maps.

The upper box of rankings contains information on Variable 1; the lower box of rankings contains information on the comparison variable.

South Koreans (53 percent) are also least receptive to having "foreigners" as neighbors, and again India (48 percent) is second. Only 10 percent of Americans object to foreigners as neighbors, and people in Switzerland and Argentina are least likely to object.

There is a huge correlation (0.899**) between not wanting neighbors who are of another race or who are foreigners. This reveals that prejudice and discrimination tend to be unidimensional phenomena—people tend to reject or accept everyone or no one. Let's pursue this idea.

Data File: **NATIONS**
Task: **Mapping**
Variable 1: **11) ANTI-RACE**
➤ Variable 2: **13) ANTI-JEW**
➤ Views: **List: Rank**

RANK	CASE NAME	VALUE
1	South Korea	58
2	India	44
3	Slovenia	40
4	Bulgaria	39
5	Nigeria	34

RANK	CASE NAME	VALUE
1	India	86
2	Turkey	59
3	Slovenia	37
4	Nigeria	34
5	Bulgaria	30

If you are continuing from the previous example, return to the variable selection screen, then select 13) ANTI-JEW as the new Variable 2.

The lower table shows the percentages in each nation who don't want Jews in their neighborhood. Indians (86 percent) overwhelmingly take this view as do the majority of Turks (59 percent). About a third of Slovenians, Nigerians, and Bulgarians don't want Jews in their neighborhood. Few Canadians (6 percent) or Americans (5 percent) take this view. But here too the correlation with objecting to persons of another race is very high (0.790**), giving further confirmation to the unidimensional nature of prejudice and the willingness to deny civil rights.

Data File: **NATIONS**
Task: **Mapping**
Variable 1: **11) ANTI-RACE**
➤ Variable 2: **14) ANTI-GAY**
➤ Views: **List: Rank**

RANK	CASE NAME	VALUE
1	South Korea	58
2	India	44
3	Slovenia	40
4	Bulgaria	39
5	Nigeria	34

RANK	CASE NAME	VALUE
1	Turkey	92
2	India	91
3	Lithuania	87
4	Russia	82
5	Belarus	79

Finally, we see very strong objections in many nations to having homosexual neighbors: 92 percent in Turkey, 91 percent in India, 82 percent in Russia, 73 percent in Nigeria, 69 percent in Japan, 38 percent in the United States, 30 percent in Canada—amazingly, South Koreans, who are most opposed to living near foreigners or members of another race, are not opposed to homosexual neighbors (4 percent).

Of course, no one objects to having women living in the neighborhood, so that can't be used as a measure of civil rights for women. But the following is a measure of gender equality.

Data File: **NATIONS**
Task: **Mapping**
Variable 1: **11) ANTI-RACE**
➤ Variable 2: **15) %FEM LEGIS**
➤ Views: **List: Rank**

RANK	CASE NAME	VALUE
1	South Korea	58
2	India	44
3	Slovenia	40
4	Bulgaria	39
5	Nigeria	34

RANK	CASE NAME	VALUE
1	Sweden	40.4
1	Norway	36.4
3	Finland	33.5
4	Denmark	33.0
5	New Zealand	29.2

This variable shows the percentage of seats in national parliaments that are held by women. Sweden (40.4 percent) is highest, the United States is relatively low with 11.2 percent, whereas in Kuwait and the United Arab Emirates none of the seats are held by women. This variable also is significantly correlated with objecting to having neighbors of another race. In this instance, of course, the correlation is negative—nations where racial prejudice is higher tend to have a lower percentage of females in the legislature.

That the battery of questions about prejudice shown above asked about willingness to have people who are different from them as neighbors reveals a universal aspect of civil rights which is based on an inherent contradiction concerning freedom: that one person's freedom can be another person's fetters. In this case, the freedom of one racial group to live in their own neighborhood curtails the freedom of others to live where they want.

Of course, for generations Americans had the freedom to exclude others from their neighborhoods, clubs, schools, buses, playgrounds, teams, beaches, hotels, theaters, restaurants, and similar settings. The most severe restrictions were imposed by whites on blacks and other nonwhites, but considerable limits also were imposed on Jews, Catholics, and various ethnic groups.

A major consequence of the civil rights movement during the 1950s and 1960s was to curtail this freedom in exchange for the freedom of others to freely associate. That is, equality was used as the standard against which to balance individual freedoms, and efforts by a group to be separated from others (to maintain *segregation*) were outlawed in many aspects of social life, including real estate.

➤ *Data File:* **HISTORY**
  ➤ *Task:* **Historical Trends**
➤ *Variables:* **66) RACE SEG**

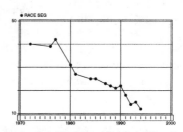

Percent who agree that whites have a right to keep African Americans out
of their neighborhoods

During the 1940's, an overwhelming majority of Americans favored separate neighborhoods for African Americans. In 1972, almost one in two Americans thought that it was acceptable for whites to exclude African Americans from their neighborhoods. By 1996, this had dropped to one in ten.

Civil rights advocates in the 1970s and 1980s pushed for the creation of affirmative action programs designed to compensate for past discrimination against minority groups. During this period, government, colleges and universities, businesses, and other groups adopted affirmative action programs to encourage the advancement of members of minority groups.

These programs have also encountered the basic contradiction: Enhancing the rights of one group may restrict the rights of another group. In 1978, the Supreme Court ruled on *Regents of the University of California v. Bakke*, one of the first cases questioning the constitutionality of such programs. Mr. Bakke, a white male, had been denied admission to medical school, while less qualified students had been admitted under a special minority program. The lawyers for Mr. Bakke alleged that the special admissions program operated to exclude him on the basis of his race. The Supreme Court agreed that the special admissions program violated the Equal Protection Clause of the Fourteenth Amendment. In recent years, voter initiatives prohibiting such programs have been placed on the ballot in several states.

Let's see how Americans feel about preferential treatment of African Americans to make up for past discrimination.

➤ *Data File:* **NES**
  ➤ *Task:* **Univariate**
➤ *Primary Variable:* **32) AFFIRM.ACT**
  ➤ *View:* **Pie**

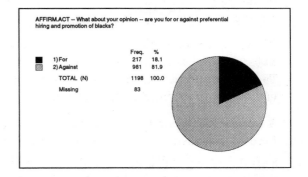

Only one out of five Americans supports preferential treatment. The results were not much different in an earlier survey question that asked about preferential treatment to make up for past discrimination against women.

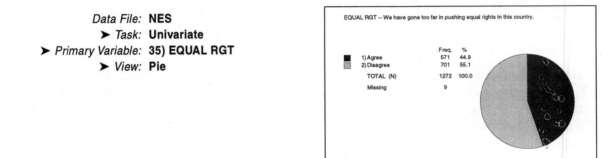

AFFIRM.ACT by RACE
Cramer's V: 0.380 **

		RACE			
		White	African-Am	Missing	TOTAL
AFFIRM.ACT	For	131	81	5	212
		12.8%	57.9%		18.2%
	Against	894	59	28	953
		87.2%	42.1%		81.8%
	Missing	66	12	5	83
	TOTAL	1025	140	38	1165
		100.0%	100.0%		

Data File: **NES**
➤ Task: **Cross-tabulation**
➤ Row Variable: **32) AFFIRM.ACT**
➤ Column Variable: **42) RACE**
➤ View: **Table**
➤ Display: **Column %**

Even among the beneficiaries of such preferential treatment (African Americans), over 40 percent are opposed. However, this doesn't mean that Americans have discarded notions of equal rights for all Americans.

Data File: **NES**
➤ Task: **Univariate**
➤ Primary Variable: **35) EQUAL RGT**
➤ View: **Pie**

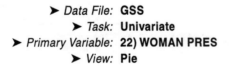

The majority do *not* agree that we have gone too far in pushing equal rights.

Earlier we saw that a good measure of gender equality could be based on the percentage of women in political office. Let's take a closer look.

➤ Data File: **GSS**
➤ Task: **Univariate**
➤ Primary Variable: **22) WOMAN PRES**
➤ View: **Pie**

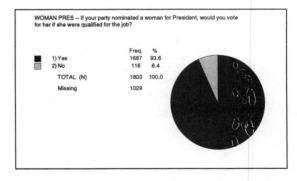

Today, more than 90 percent of Americans say they would vote for a woman for president. That wasn't always so. When this question was asked in the 1930s, only about one-third of Americans would vote for a woman for president. Let's look at the trend.

➤ *Data File:* **HISTORY**
    ➤ *Task:* **Historical Trends**
➤ *Variables:* **29) %FEM PRES**

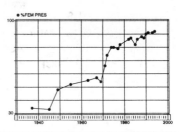

Percent who would vote for woman for president (survey data)

Your turn.

Exercise 5: Civil Rights: Equality

Part III

GOVERNMENT AND THE INDIVIDUAL

The basis of political freedom is simple to identify and very difficult to maintain: We the People. But who are the people? Are they everyone? Or only everyone who cares? Or are they only those who try to influence political decisions? What is consent? Do elections provide an adequate measure of it? Or should elected officials simply vote according to the polls? If not, how should they represent us? How shall governments distinguish between the abiding interests of the people and our momentary enthusiasms? As we shall see, there are no clear or final answers to these questions. But only as we constantly apply them to our political realities, can we sustain a free society.

EXERCISE 6

PUBLIC OPINION AND POLITICAL SOCIALIZATION

About things on which the public thinks long it commonly attains to think right.

SAMUEL JOHNSON, 1778

Tasks: Univariate, Cross-Tabulation, Mapping
Data Files: GSS, STATES

The opinion poll (or survey) has become an essential part of our political life offering constant reflections of the opinions, interests, anxieties, and antagonisms of the American public. Yet, not so many years ago there were no polls and no one could really know how the public felt about anything. The first reliable pre-election polls of voters were conducted in 1936 by George Gallup, founder of the Gallup Poll, and by his rival Elmo Roper, founder of the Roper Poll. Then, as now, the polls often revealed surprises—if it were easy to gauge public opinion, no one would pay the large sums needed to conduct a trustworthy survey.

In Exercise 3 you learned that public opinion polls work because they are based on *random samples* of sufficient size. However, even when the results are based on large, random samples, they can be very misleading. Consequently, some of the "surprises" revealed by surveys don't really mean what they appear to mean.

Suppose we want to know how Americans feel about legal abortions.

➤ *Data File:* **GSS**
➤ *Task:* **Univariate**
➤ *Primary Variable:* **41) ABORT.HLTH**
➤ *View:* **Pie**

ABORT.HLTH -- LEGAL ABORTION: If the woman's own health is seriously endangered by the pregnancy?

		Freq.	%
■	1) Approve	1578	87.9
▨	2) Disapprove	218	12.1
	TOTAL (N)	1796	100.0
	Missing	1036	

Someone might look at these results and report that nearly all Americans (87.9 percent) favor allowing abortions to be legal. Clearly, it is true that about 9 Americans out of 10 favor allowing abortions when a woman's own health is seriously endangered by the pregnancy. (Notice that the question was not asked of all respondents; thus, data are missing on the attitudes of 1,036 persons. This does not weaken our confidence in the results because random techniques were used not only to select the total sample but also to decide which members of the sample were asked this question.)

However, before we rush to report the huge public support for abortion, notice that the question is not about abortion in general, but about abortions for a very specific reason. Perhaps Americans line up rather differently when the reason for an abortion is less compelling than to save the woman's life?

Data File: **GSS**
Task: **Univariate**
➤ *Primary Variable:* **40) ABORT.WANT**
➤ *View:* **Pie**

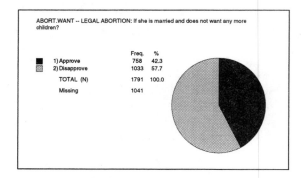

Based on these results alone, someone might report that most Americans (57.7 percent) oppose abortion. Here, again, abortion opinions are linked to a very specific circumstance, a married woman who does not want any more children. So, what do Americans think about abortion in general?

Data File: **GSS**
Task: **Univariate**
➤ *Primary Variable:* **42) ABORT ANY**
➤ *View:* **Pie**

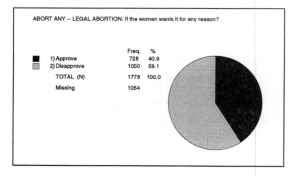

When asked whether abortions ought to be legal "if the woman wants it for any reason," most Americans (59.1 percent) disapprove.

So, in response to the question "Do Americans favor or oppose abortion?" the most accurate answer is "It depends."

That public opinion would vary greatly across these three questions may seem obvious. But even far more subtle differences can cause large shifts in how people answer.

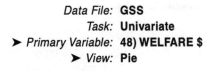

Data File: **GSS**
Task: **Univariate**
➤ *Primary Variable:* **48) WELFARE $**
➤ *View:* **Pie**

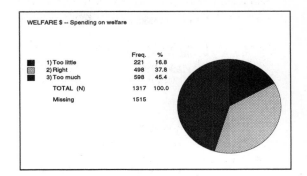

WELFARE $ -- Spending on welfare

		Freq.	%
■	1) Too little	221	16.8
▨	2) Right	498	37.8
■	3) Too much	598	45.4
	TOTAL (N)	1317	100.0
	Missing	1515	

Here we see public opposition to welfare. Only 16.8 percent think the government is spending too little money on welfare, while nearly half (45.4 percent) think the government is spending too much. Results like these have stimulated many accusations that Americans lack compassion, that they don't care what happens to poor people.

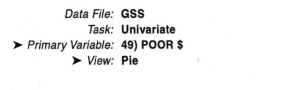

Data File: **GSS**
Task: **Univariate**
➤ *Primary Variable:* **49) POOR $**
➤ *View:* **Pie**

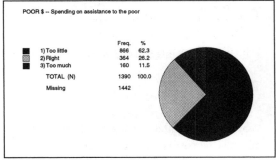

POOR $ -- Spending on assistance to the poor

		Freq.	%
■	1) Too little	866	62.3
▨	2) Right	364	26.2
■	3) Too much	160	11.5
	TOTAL (N)	1390	100.0
	Missing	1442	

But if that's so, what are we to make of this result? When asked about spending on assistance to the poor rather than spending on welfare, more than half (62.3 percent) of Americans responded that the government is spending too little! Only about 1 in 10 thought current spending is too high. How would you explain these "conflicting" results?

Suppose that rather than asking why people give such different answers to these two questions, we asked a far more basic question: *How do people come to hold any of the opinions and beliefs that they do?*

There are, of course, many answers to that question because many factors influence our opinions. However, there is a very general and basic difference between people in the way they assess political issues. Some people form their political opinions issue by issue, and surveys reveal very little consistency among their opinions. That is, some people take a very liberal position on one issue, a very conservative position on another, and a moderate position on a third. However, when we identify liberal and conservative positions on issues, we are assuming that there exist consistent sets of political opinions. Such sets are called **political ideologies**.

Unlike people who form their opinions issue by issue, others have acquired and developed a general frame of reference, an ideology, against which to judge specific issues as they arise. In American politics the labels "liberal," "moderate," and "conservative" identify the major ideologies.

Data File: **GSS**
Task: **Univariate**
➤ Primary Variable: **5) LIB./CONS.**
➤ View: **Pie**

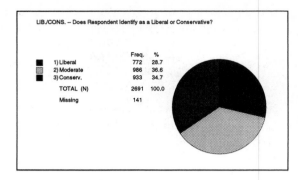

LIB./CONS. -- Does Respondent Identify as a Liberal or Conservative?

	Freq.	%
1) Liberal	772	28.7
2) Moderate	986	36.6
3) Conserv.	933	34.7
TOTAL (N)	2691	100.0
Missing	141	

Today, liberals (28.7 percent) are outnumbered by conservatives (34.7 percent) and by moderates (36.6 percent). Now let's see how ideology influences attitudes about abortion.

Data File: **GSS**
➤ Task: **Cross-tabulation**
➤ Row Variable: **40) ABORT.WANT**
➤ Column Variable: **5) LIB./CONS.**
➤ View: **Table**
➤ Display: **Column %**

ABORT.WANT by LIB./CONS.
Cramer's V: 0.266 **

		LIB./CONS.				
		Liberal	Moderate	Conserv.	Missing	TOTAL
ABORT.WANT	Approve	316	250	159	33	725
		60.5%	41.6%	27.8%		42.8%
	Disapprove	206	351	412	64	969
		39.5%	58.4%	72.2%		57.2%
	Missing	250	385	.	44	1041
	TOTAL	522	601	571	141	1694
		100.0%	100.0%	100.0%		

Very strongly! Liberals are far more likely than conservatives to approve of abortions being legal for married women who don't want any more children. Put another way, if a person says he or she is liberal the odds are about 3 to 2 that he or she will approve of abortions in this circumstance, whereas for those who say they are conservatives the odds are about 3 to 1 in the other direction. And, of course, differences this great in a sample this large are highly significant.

Notice, however, that many Americans hold views on this issue that are not a reflection of their ideology. That is, many liberals oppose abortion in this circumstance, while many conservatives support it. Thus, political scientists acknowledge that ideology plays only a limited role in American politics—and probably a far more limited role than it does in some other nations. In addition, ideology plays a more important role on some issues than on others.

But where do people get their political opinions, especially their political ideologies? The answer is, of course, that we learn them from others and from experience. And this learning process often is referred to as political socialization.

Political socialization is the complex process by which individuals become aware of politics, learn political facts, and form their political views. Although political socialization helps to explain how people acquire their opinions on *specific* issues, it is especially useful for examining how people acquire a general perspective or political ideology. Political scientists take a special interest in political socialization, paying particular attention to **agents of socialization**, the primary sources of political socialization.

Our political socialization begins early as our families are the initial agents of our socialization. Considerable research shows that people tend to resemble their parents in terms of their political ideologies and interest. This is especially true of party preferences. Democrats tend to raise Democrats, while the children of Republicans tend to grow up as Republicans.

But, although childhood influences may be an important source of political socialization, they are soon reinforced or countermanded by other primary agents of socialization: school, church, work, region, and community. In addition to these, our political outlooks are greatly shaped by our life experiences. Here's an example:

Data File: **GSS**
Task: **Cross-tabulation**
➤ Row Variable: **5) LIB./CONS.**
➤ Column Variable: **9) EVER UNEMP**
➤ View: **Table**
➤ Display: **Column %**

LIB./CONS.   by   EVER UNEMP
Cramer's V: 0.092 **

		EVER UNEMP			
		Yes	No	Missing	TOTAL
LIB./CONS.	Liberal	179	301	292	480
		32.7%	23.9%		26.6%
	Moderate	187	496	303	683
		34.2%	39.4%		37.8%
	Conserv.	181	461	291	642
		33.1%	36.6%		35.6%
	Missing	33	58	50	141
	TOTAL	547	1258	936	1805
		100.0%	100.0%		

People who have been unemployed are more likely to be liberals than are those who have never been out of work, and they are less likely to be conservatives. Put another way, people who have been unemployed are about equally likely to be liberals (32.7 percent) as to be conservatives (33.1 percent), but those who never have been unemployed are far more likely to be conservatives (36.6 percent) than to be liberals (23.9 percent).

Another aspect of life experience that is apt to influence ideology is one's racial or ethnic background.

Data File: **GSS**
Task: **Cross-tabulation**
Row Variable: **5) LIB./CONS.**
➤ Column Variable: **3) WH/AFR.AM**
➤ View: **Table**
➤ Display: **Column %**

LIB./CONS.   by   WH/AFR.AM
Cramer's V: 0.077 **

		WH/AFR.AM			
		White	African-Am	Missing	TOTAL
LIB./CONS.	Liberal	596	113	63	709
		27.8%	30.1%		28.1%
	Moderate	756	162	68	918
		35.3%	43.1%		36.4%
	Conserv.	792	101	40	893
		36.9%	26.9%		35.4%
	Missing	97	24	20	141
	TOTAL	2144	376	191	2520
		100.0%	100.0%		

Race does shape political ideologies. But the differences are smaller than many would have expected. Among Whites, conservatives modestly outnumber liberals; among African Americans, liberals (30.1 percent) modestly outnumber conservatives (26.9 percent).

Another factor shaping our political ideologies is *where* we live.

Data File: **GSS**

Task: **Cross-tabulation**

Row Variable: **5) LIB./CONS.**

➤ Column Variable: **65) REGION**

➤ View: **Table**

➤ Display: **Column %**

LIB./CONS.   by   REGION
Cramer's V: 0.074 **

		REGION				
		East	Midwest	South	West	TOTAL
L I B . / C O N S .	Liberal	164	183	238	187	772
		30.8%	27.2%	24.8%	35.4%	28.7%
	Moderate	212	258	351	165	986
		39.8%	38.3%	36.6%	31.3%	36.6%
	Conserv.	156	232	369	176	933
		29.3%	34.5%	38.5%	33.3%	34.7%
	Missing	37	23	63	18	141
	TOTAL	532	673	958	528	2691
		100.0%	100.0%	100.0%	100.0%	

Southerners are the least apt to identify themselves as liberals, and Westerners are the most likely. Southerners are the most likely to say they are conservatives. Here, too, although the differences are statistically significant, they are modest.

An important agent of political socialization is the church.

Data File: **GSS**

Task: **Cross-tabulation**

Row Variable: **5) LIB./CONS.**

➤ Column Variable: **64) RELIGION**

➤ View: **Table**

➤ Display: **Column %**

LIB./CONS.   by   RELIGION
Cramer's V: 0.127 **

		RELIGION					
		Cons.Prot.	Lib.Prot.	Catholic	None	Missing	TOTAL
L I B . / C O N S .	Liberal	170	140	189	165	108	664
		22.5%	24.5%	28.6%	43.7%		28.1%
	Moderate	276	225	251	135	99	887
		36.5%	39.3%	38.0%	35.7%		37.5%
	Conserv.	310	207	220	78	118	815
		41.0%	36.2%	33.3%	20.6%		34.4%
	Missing	53	10	45	18	15	141
	TOTAL	756	572	660	378	340	2366
		100.0%	100.0%	100.0%	100.0%		

Here we see that members of conservative Protestant denominations (Baptists or Assemblies of God, for example) are those most apt to identify themselves as political conservatives. However, they are not much more apt to do so than are members of liberal Protestant denominations (Methodists or Episcopalians, for example) or Catholics. In all three denominational groupings, conservatives outnumber liberals. But this pattern is sharply reversed among those who say they have no religious preference.

A person's gender is also an important element of socialization. Let's see if this has any effect on political views.

Data File: **GSS**

Task: **Cross-tabulation**

Row Variable: **5) LIB./CONS.**

➤ Column Variable: **61) SEX**

➤ View: **Table**

➤ Display: **Column %**

LIB./CONS.   by   SEX
Cramer's V: 0.068 **

		SEX		
		Male	Female	TOTAL
L I B . / C O N S .	Liberal	314	458	772
		26.5%	30.5%	28.7%
	Moderate	419	567	986
		35.3%	37.7%	36.6%
	Conserv.	454	479	933
		38.2%	31.8%	34.7%
	Missing	45	96	141
	TOTAL	1187	1504	2691
		100.0%	100.0%	

We can see that the respondent's gender has a relatively weak effect.

Part III: Government and the Individual

Let's see how stable these attitudes are.

Data File: **GSS**

Task: **Cross-tabulation**

Row Variable: **5) LIB./CONS.**

➤ Column Variable: **66) AGE**

➤ View: **Table**

➤ Display: **Column %**

LIB./CONS.   by   AGE
Cramer's V: 0.077 **

		AGE						
		Under 30	30-39	40-49	50-64	65 & Over	Missing	TOTAL
LIB./CONS.	Liberal	180	193	166	134	99	0	772
		35.4%	29.5%	29.7%	25.8%	22.1%		28.7%
	Moderate	192	228	189	199	174	4	982
		37.8%	34.9%	33.9%	38.3%	38.8%		36.5%
	Conserv.	136	233	203	186	175	0	933
		26.8%	35.6%	36.4%	35.8%	39.1%		34.7%
	Missing	29	33	22	26	31	0	141
	TOTAL	508	654	558	519	448	4	2687
		100.0%	100.0%	100.0%	100.0%	100.0%		

The older the individual, the less likely he or she is to be liberal and the more likely to be conservative. This suggests that these political attitudes may change as a person gets older. This would be an aging effect. However, these data are not adequate to establish that a change in opinion occurs with aging. It also is possible that today's elderly were more conservative in their youth and have remained conservative throughout their lifetimes. This would be a generational effect. In order to distinguish between an aging effect and a generational effect, we would need to follow the *same respondents* over their lifetimes. A cross-sectional survey, like the General Social Survey, can tell us only that older people differ from younger people.

Your turn.

EXERCISE 7

THE MEDIA

Where the press is free and every[one] able to read, all is safe.

THOMAS JEFFERSON, 1816

Tasks: Mapping, Univariate, Cross-Tabulation, Historical Trends
Data Files: NATIONS, NES, GSS, HISTORY

ew Americans have ever attended a political gathering, met a candidate for national office, or observed a session of an elected body—neither Congress nor their local city council. For most Americans, politics is a media event, and in that sense they resemble the old-time cowboy comedian Will Rogers who liked to claim "All I know is what I read in the papers."

For generations, newspapers were the only important mass medium—newsmagazines are far more recent. *Time* was founded in 1923 but did not gain much circulation during its first few years of operation, and *Newsweek* did not appear until several years later. The many magazines of political opinion, such as *National Review, Nation, New Republic,* and *American Spectator,* are much more recent and have only small circulations—*National Review* is the largest but has a total circulation of less than 200,000. By the 1930s, radio competed with the print media to bring the news, to offer live broadcasts of political conventions, and to report returns on election nights. Following World War II, television soon became the dominant medium—the first political conventions were televised in 1948, and that also was the first time a computer (weighing many tons) was used on election night.

Today, Americans gain their knowledge and impressions of politics from both the print and electronic media. The same is true in most of the world.

➤ *Data File:* **NATIONS**
➤ *Task:* **Mapping**
➤ *Variable 1:* **30) NEWSPAPERS**
➤ *View:* **List: Rank**

RANK	CASE NAME	VALUE
1	Norway	607
2	Japan	576
3	Croatia	575
4	Iceland	515
5	Sweden	483
6	Finland	473
7	Austria	472
8	Switzerland	409
9	South Korea	404
10	Kuwait	401

Newspaper readership differs a lot among these nations. In Norway, 607 newspapers are circulated daily for every 1,000 persons. By comparison, newspaper readership is rather low in the United States,

111

about one paper for every four persons. However, newspaper circulation once was much higher in the United States.

> *Data File:* **HISTORY**
> > *Task:* **Historical Trends**
> *Variables:* **25) NEWS/100**

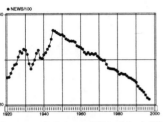

Newspaper circulation per 100 population in U.S.

One reason newspaper readership has declined in the United States, and probably in some other nations as well, is the prevalence of television.

> *Data File:* **NATIONS**
> > *Task:* **Mapping**
> *Variable 1:* **31) TELEVISION**
> > *View:* **List: Rank**

RANK	CASE NAME	VALUE
1	United States	81.73
2	Malta	73.91
3	Canada	68.26
4	Japan	68.00
5	Oman	66.78
6	France	58.89
7	Germany	55.75
8	Denmark	53.59
9	New Zealand	51.93
10	Finland	51.12

The United States leads the world in the number of television sets per 100 persons, with 81.73. Next is Malta, followed by Canada, Japan, and Oman. In contrast, there are few television sets in Nigeria (4.24) and India (4.04).

> *Data File:* **HISTORY**
> > *Task:* **Historical Trends**
> *Variables:* **26) TV/100HH**

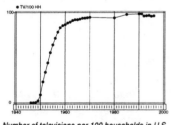

Number of televisions per 100 households in U.S.

The spread of television sets in the United States was amazingly rapid. In 1949 hardly anyone had a set, whereas in 1959 almost everyone did.

Of course, many people with TV sets don't watch television news.

➤ *Data File:* **NES**
➤ *Task:* **Univariate**
➤ *Primary Variable:* **6) TV NEWS?**
➤ *View:* **Pie**

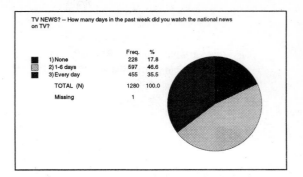

TV NEWS? -- How many days in the past week did you watch the national news on TV?

	Freq.	%
1) None	228	17.8
2) 1-6 days	597	46.6
3) Every day	455	35.5
TOTAL (N)	1280	100.0
Missing	1	

About a third of Americans say they watch TV news every day.

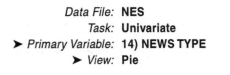

Data File: **NES**
Task: **Univariate**
➤ *Primary Variable:* **7) READ PAPER**
➤ *View:* **Pie**

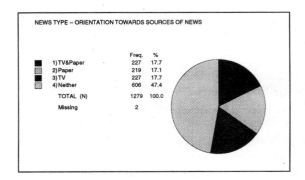

READ PAPER -- How many days in the past week did you read a daily newspaper?

	Freq.	%
1) Every day	447	34.9
2) 1-6 days	597	46.6
3) None	236	18.4
TOTAL (N)	1280	100.0
Missing	1	

About the same number of Americans watch TV news daily as read a daily newspaper.

Data File: **NES**
Task: **Univariate**
➤ *Primary Variable:* **14) NEWS TYPE**
➤ *View:* **Pie**

NEWS TYPE -- ORIENTATION TOWARDS SOURCES OF NEWS

	Freq.	%
1) TV&Paper	227	17.7
2) Paper	219	17.1
3) TV	227	17.7
4) Neither	606	47.4
TOTAL (N)	1279	100.0
Missing	2	

Here the questions about watching TV news and reading newspapers have been combined to produce four basic types of persons. The first consists of those who read newspapers and watch TV news every day. They make up about 18 percent of the adult population. The second type only reads the newspapers daily, watching TV news less often. They are about 17 percent of Americans. The third type watches TV news daily but reads the paper less often. Finally, the fourth type consists of those who do not watch TV news or read a newspaper daily—about half of the public.

Does it matter if one both watches the TV news and reads the newspaper in terms of being informed about politics?

Data File: **NES**
➤ Task: **Cross-tabulation**
➤ Row Variable: **5) INFORMED?**
➤ Column Variable: **14) NEWS TYPE**
➤ View: **Table**
➤ Display: **Column %**

INFORMED? by NEWS TYPE
Cramer's V: 0.241 **

		TV&Paper	Paper	TV	Neither	Missing	TOTAL
INFORMED?	High	123	110	89	160	0	482
		54.2%	50.2%	39.2%	26.4%		37.7%
	Aver/Low	104	109	138	446	2	797
		45.8%	49.8%	60.8%	73.6%		62.3%
	TOTAL	227	219	227	606	2	1279
		100.0%	100.0%	100.0%	100.0%		

Yes! A majority of those who both read newspapers and watch TV news daily were rated as highly informed by the interviewers. However, those who rely primarily on the newspaper were equally likely to be highly informed. But those who rely on TV news were much less apt to be highly informed (39.2 percent). Not surprisingly, most of those who neither read the paper nor watch TV news daily were rated as less then highly informed.

But what about credibility? The effects of the news media depend, at least in part, on how much confidence readers and viewers place in them.

➤ Data File: **NATIONS**
➤ Task: **Mapping**
➤ Variable 1: **22) PRESS?**
➤ View: **List: Rank**

RANK	CASE NAME	VALUE
1	Nigeria	75
2	Estonia	73
3	Lithuania	67
4	South Korea	66
5	India	63
6	Latvia	60
7	South Africa	59
8	United States	56
8	China	56
10	Brazil	55

People in each nation were asked how much confidence they had in the press. Here we see the percentage who said they had at least some confidence in the press as compared with little or no confidence. Three of four people in Nigeria said they had at least some confidence in the press. The United States and China are tied, with 56 percent saying they had some confidence. Keeping in mind that this is the most generous estimate of confidence in the press, it would appear that large numbers of people simply don't trust what they read in the papers, hear on the radio, or see on TV. In Great Britain only 14 percent say they have some confidence in the press as do 18 percent in Austria.

➤ Data File: **HISTORY**
➤ Task: **Historical Trends**
➤ Variables: **37) CONF.PRESS**

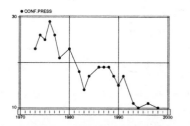

Percent with great deal of confidence in the press (survey data)

Confidence in the press has been declining in the United States.

➤ *Data File:* **GSS**
➤ *Task:* **Cross-tabulation**
➤ *Row Variable:* **33) PRESS?**
➤ *Column Variable:* **65) REGION**
➤ *View:* **Table**
➤ *Display:* **Column %**

PRESS? by REGION
Cramer's V: 0.057

		REGION				
		East	Midwest	South	West	TOTAL
PRESS?	Some conf	220	273	369	192	1054
		60.3%	59.3%	54.4%	53.5%	56.6%
	Low conf	145	187	309	167	808
		39.7%	40.7%	45.6%	46.5%	43.4%
	Missing	204	236	343	187	970
	TOTAL	365	460	678	359	1862
		100.0%	100.0%	100.0%	100.0%	

There is no significant regional effect on confidence in the press.

In addition to watching TV and reading the paper, many people listen to talk shows on the radio.

➤ *Data File:* **NES**
➤ *Task:* **Univariate**
➤ *Primary Variable:* **8) CALL RADIO**
➤ *View:* **Pie**

CALL RADIO -- There are a number of programs on the radio in which people call in to voice their opinions about politics. Did you ever listen to political talk radio programs of this type?

		Freq.	%
■	1) Yes	429	33.5
▨	2) No	852	66.5
	TOTAL (N)	1281	100.0

We find that a third of Americans listen to radio talk shows.

The three traditional news media sources over the past 50 years have been newspapers, TV, and radio. The Internet has now joined these traditional news sources. Many newspapers and television outlets have expanded to include Internet sites. Candidates, interest groups, and the political parties now use the Internet to bring their messages directly to the public.

Now you will have a chance to find out more about the audience for different types of media and what impact the media have on political opinions.

Your turn.

WORKSHEET

EXERCISE 7

NAME:

COURSE:

DATE:

REVIEW QUESTIONS

Based on the first part of this exercise, answer True or False to the following items:

Because it can provide live video, TV is more effective than newspapers in communicating political information.	T	F
Newspaper circulation is increasing, primarily because Americans are becoming more educated.	T	F
A majority of Americans watch TV news every day.	T	F
Confidence in the press has been declining in the United States.	T	F
The British have less confidence in the press than do Americans.	T	F

EXPLORIT QUESTIONS

1. For the media to have any impact, someone must read, or listen to, or watch the medium. Let's see how education and age influence what and how much people read or watch.

    ➤ *Data File:* **NES**
    ➤ *Task:* **Cross-tabulation**
    ➤ *Row Variable:* **7) READ PAPER**
    ➤ *Column Variable:* **48) EDUCATION**
    ➤ *View:* **Table**
    ➤ *Display:* **Column %**

	NOT HS GRAD	HS GRAD	SOME COL	COLL.GRAD.
% who read the paper every day	_____%	_____%	_____%	_____%

What is the value of V for this table?   V = _____

Is it statistically significant?   Yes   No

WORKSHEET

EXERCISE 7

Data File: **NES**
Task: **Cross-tabulation**
➤ Row Variable: **6) TV NEWS?**
➤ Column Variable: **48) EDUCATION**
➤ View: **Table**
➤ Display: **Column %**

	NOT HS GRAD	HS GRAD	SOME COL	COLL.GRAD.
% who watch TV news daily (Note: This is the third row in the table.)	_____%	_____%	_____%	_____%

What is the value of V for this table? V = _____

Is it statistically significant? Yes   No

Data File: **NES**
Task: **Cross-tabulation**
➤ Row Variable: **7) READ PAPER**
➤ Column Variable: **47) AGE**
➤ View: **Table**
➤ Display: **Column %**

	UNDER 30	30–39	40–49	50–64	OVER 64
% who read the paper every day	_____%	_____%	_____%	_____%	_____%

What is the value of V for this table? V = _____

Is it statistically significant? Yes   No

Data File: **NES**
Task: **Cross-tabulation**
➤ Row Variable: **6) TV NEWS?**
➤ Column Variable: **47) AGE**
➤ View: **Table**
➤ Display: **Column %**

	UNDER 30	30–39	40–49	50–64	OVER 64
% who watch TV news daily	_____%	_____%	_____%	_____%	_____%

What is the value of V for this table?   V = _____

Is it statistically significant?   Yes   No

Answer True or False to the following items:

The higher an individual's education, the more likely he or she is to watch TV
news daily.   T   F

The higher an individual's education, the more likely he or she is to read the
newspaper daily.   T   F

Older people are more likely to read the newspaper every day than are
younger people.   T   F

Younger people are more likely to watch TV news daily than are older people.   T   F

2. There are several variables that provide additional information about the respondent's political knowl-
    edge. Included in these is awareness, measured in 1998, of the two major contenders for the 2000
    Democratic nomination for president, Vice President Al Gore and New Jersey Senator Bill Bradley.
    Let's see if reading the paper or watching TV news made any difference in awareness of these two
    candidates.

> Data File: **NES**
> Task: **Cross-tabulation**
> ➤ Row Variable: **27) GORE KNOW**
> ➤ Column Variable: **7) READ PAPER**
> ➤ View: **Table**
> ➤ Display: **Column %**

What is the value of V for this table?   V = _____

Is it statistically significant?   Yes   No

If significant, is this a moderate or weak relationship?   Moderate   Weak

> Row Variable: **27) GORE KNOW**
> ➤ Column Variable: **6) TV NEWS?**
> ➤ View: **Table**
> ➤ Display: **Column %**

What is the value of V for this table?   V = _____

Is it statistically significant?   Yes   No

If significant, is this a moderate or weak relationship?   Moderate   Weak

➤ *Row Variable:*   **30) BRAD. KNOW**
➤ *Column Variable:*   **7) READ PAPER**
     ➤ *View:*   **Table**
     ➤ *Display:*   **Column %**

What is the value of V for this table?   V = _____

Is it statistically significant?   Yes   No

If significant, is this a moderate or weak relationship?   Moderate   Weak

Row Variable: **30) BRAD. KNOW**
➤ *Column Variable:*   **6) TV NEWS?**
     ➤ *View:*   **Table**
     ➤ *Display:*   **Column %**

What is the value of V for this table?   V = _____

Is it statistically significant?   Yes   No

If significant, is this a moderate or weak relationship?   Moderate   Weak

Summarize what these results suggest about the relative impact of newspapers and TV news on the respondent's knowledge.

3. Previously we saw that those who both read newspapers and watched TV news daily were better informed about politics. Let's see how daily media usage affects the likelihood that people will talk about politics.

         Data File: **NES**
         Task: **Cross-tabulation**
➤ *Row Variable:*   **11) TALK POL?**
➤ *Column Variable:*   **14) NEWS TYPE**
     ➤ *View:*   **Table**
     ➤ *Display:*   **Column %**

	TV & PAPER	PAPER	TV	NEITHER
% who talk politics	_____%	_____%	_____%	_____%

What is the value of V for this table?   V = _____

Is it statistically significant?   Yes   No

4. Some critics of media coverage of government contend that the media only present the negative side of the story, such as when a government program is not working. If these critics are correct, then people who frequently watch TV news and read newspapers should be less trusting of the government than other Americans. Other pundits might contend that people who are very distrustful of the government would not bother watching TV news or reading the newspaper, since these Americans would be less interested in news about a government they distrusted. Finally, a third group of scholars might speculate that since most Americans tend to distrust the government, media usage would have little to no influence on any individual's evaluation of the government. Let's see which of these three possible explanations might be correct.

> Data File: **NES**
> Task: **Cross-tabulation**
> ➤ Row Variable: **22) TRUST GOV**
> ➤ Column Variable: **14) NEWS TYPE**
> ➤ View: **Table**
> ➤ Display: **Column %**

	TV & PAPER	PAPER	TV	NEITHER
% some/never trust the government	_____%	_____%	_____%	_____%

What is the value of V for this table?   V = _____

Is it statistically significant?   Yes   No

Which of the three contending explanations is best supported by the survey data?

EXERCISE 8

POLITICAL PARTICIPATION

Politics ought to be the part-time profession of every citizen.

DWIGHT D. EISENHOWER, 1954

Tasks: Mapping, Univariate, Cross-Tabulation, Historical Trends, Auto-Analyzer
Data Files: NATIONS, NES, STATES, HISTORY

Political participation refers to the actions by ordinary citizens in pursuit of their political goals. The usual modes of participation are conventional—they are legal and regarded as appropriate. For example, voting, signing petitions, or campaigning on behalf of candidates or issues are conventional modes of political participation (at least they are in democratic nations). Sometimes, however, groups utilize unconventional means in pursuit of their goals. These are unusual modes of participation, often outside the law and in defiance of the government or social conventions—these include protests, demonstrations, even rebellions. Keep in mind too, as noted above, what are conventional means of political participation in some nations, such as free elections, are unavailable in others. However, while many people (usually the overwhelming majority) do not engage in unconventional political participation, many also fail to utilize conventional modes of participation. For example, many people don't bother to vote.

Let's begin with measures of unconventional participation.

> *Data File:* **NATIONS**
> *Task:* **Mapping**
> *Variable 1:* **8) SIT-INS**
> *View:* **List: Rank**

RANK	CASE NAME	VALUE
1	South Korea	10.7
2	Italy	9.7
3	France	7.9
4	Mexico	5.2
5	Belgium	4.3
6	Chile	4.2
7	Poland	3.8
8	Canada	3.0
9	Spain	2.9
10	Argentina	2.7

Few people in any of these nations have "occupied buildings or factories" as an act of direct political action. South Koreans are highest (10.7 percent), closely followed by the Italians (9.7 percent) and the French (7.9 percent). Two percent of Americans, Brazilians, and the Irish have done so. Only one person out of a thousand has taken part in a "sit-in" in Hungary.

Data File: **NATIONS**
Task: **Mapping**
➤ Variable 1: **39) FIGHT COPS**
➤ View: **List: Rank**

RANK	CASE NAME	VALUE
1	Slovak Republic	78.0
2	Czech Republic	77.3
3	Finland	74.9
4	Mexico	73.0
5	Latvia	71.7
6	Belarus	71.0
7	Lithuania	68.8
8	South Korea	66.6
9	Russia	61.6
10	Netherlands	60.7

In contrast, large numbers in most countries think it sometimes is justified to fight with the police—about three-fourths of those in the Slovak and the Czech Republics, Finland, and Mexico hold this view of illegal political expression. About half of Americans also think it sometimes is justified to battle the cops, as do Italians, Poles, Canadians, and the French. Small minorities expressed this opinion in Denmark, Romania, and Brazil.

Data File: **NATIONS**
Task: **Mapping**
➤ Variable 1: **5) PERSUASION**
➤ View: **List: Rank**

RANK	CASE NAME	VALUE
1	Denmark	34.0
2	Lithuania	32.6
3	Romania	31.6
4	Hungary	30.2
5	Belarus	27.5
6	Bulgaria	26.9
7	Nigeria	26.1
8	Argentina	24.2
9	Chile	23.5
10	Estonia	23.2

Turning to more conventional modes of participation, here we see the percentage in each nation who often try to persuade others to accept their political views. In no nation is this something that most people do often. Denmark is highest with 34 percent, only 16.9 percent of Americans said they did this often, and fewer than one in ten did so in Great Britain, France, India, Japan, and Finland.

Data File: **NATIONS**
Task: **Mapping**
➤ Variable 1: **38) % VOTED**
➤ View: **List: Rank**

RANK	CASE NAME	VALUE
1	Malta	98.0
2	Uruguay	96.1
3	Indonesia	92.8
4	Cambodia	88.8
5	Angola	88.3
6	Iceland	87.8
7	Italy	87.3
8	Somalia	87.1
9	Western Samoa	86.3
10	South Africa	85.5

Here we see the percentage of the population who voted in the most recent national election (although the percentages are quite stable from one election to the next). In many nations, more than 80 percent vote (98 percent in Malta). Voter turnout is about 50 percent in the United States. In the close and heated election of 2000, voter turnout was approximately 51 percent in the United States.

Much mention is made in the press about low voter turnouts in the United States, but the reasons are rather obvious. For one thing, because of the frequency of state and local elections, Americans are asked to vote far more often than are people in most nations; even so, the American voter usually faces a much longer and far more complex ballot than do most voters—far more American offices are elective, and in many nations there are no bond issues or initiatives on the ballot. A second reason is registration. Americans must register themselves to vote whereas in many other nations the government sees to it that everyone is registered. A third reason is that some nations—including Australia and Belgium—have compulsory voting laws. Citizens who fail to vote must pay a fine or are subject to a special tax. Finally, many critics believe that American voters lack motivation to vote because their choices are limited to two parties.

➤ *Data File:* **NES**
➤ *Task:* **Univariate**
➤ *Primary Variable:* **12) BUTTON**
➤ *View:* **Pie**

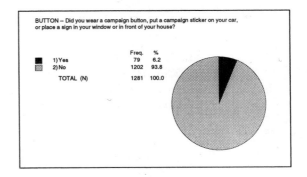

BUTTON -- Did you wear a campaign button, put a campaign sticker on your car, or place a sign in your window or in front of your house?

		Freq.	%
■	1) Yes	79	6.2
▦	2) No	1202	93.8
	TOTAL (N)	1281	100.0

Until recently, campaign buttons, bumper stickers, and yard signs were widely used forms of American political expression. As election day neared, a substantial number of people wore buttons in support of candidates (especially presidential candidates) and automobile bumpers offered an instant education in partisan politics. But in the past several years, bumper stickers and campaign buttons are much less common. In fact, only 6 percent reported wearing a button, displaying a bumper sticker, or putting a sign in their window or yard.

Data File: **NES**
Task: **Univariate**
➤ *Primary Variable:* **13) CANDID.$**
➤ *View:* **Pie**

CANDID.$ -- Did you give money to an individual candidate running for public office?

		Freq.	%
■	1) Yes	62	4.8
▦	2) No	1217	95.2
	TOTAL (N)	1279	100.0
	Missing	2	

One American in 20 reported that he or she had made a campaign contribution to a candidate for political office during the previous year.

Data File: **NES**
Task: **Univariate**
➤ Primary Variable: **19) PARTY $**
➤ View: **Pie**

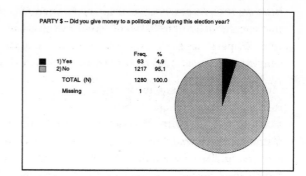

PARTY $ -- Did you give money to a political party during this election year?

		Freq.	%
■	1) Yes	63	4.9
▨	2) No	1217	95.1
	TOTAL (N)	1280	100.0
	Missing	1	

The same number of Americans had given money to a political party. How, then, does the average American participate in politics?

Data File: **NES**
Task: **Univariate**
➤ Primary Variable: **11) TALK POL?**
➤ View: **Pie**

TALK POL? -- During the campaign, did you talk to any people and try to show them why they should vote for or against one of the parties or candidates?

		Freq.	%
■	1) Yes	256	20.0
▨	2) No	1024	80.0
	TOTAL (N)	1280	100.0
	Missing	1	

About one in five Americans tries to influence the political views of others in informal conversations.

Data File: **NES**
Task: **Univariate**
➤ Primary Variable: **1) VOTE?**
➤ View: **Pie**

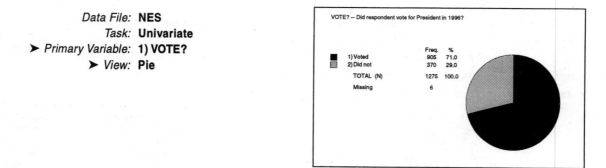

VOTE? -- Did respondent vote for President in 1996?

		Freq.	%
■	1) Voted	905	71.0
▨	2) Did not	370	29.0
	TOTAL (N)	1275	100.0
	Missing	6	

The most common and conventional form of political participation in the United States is voting. Here we see the percentage who said they voted, based on the National Election Study, conducted in 1998, two years after the election. The NES found that 71.0 percent claimed to have voted in the 1996 election, but in fact, only 49.8 percent voted.

There are three reasons for the overestimate. One is that some people who meant to vote and often vote, but who didn't vote this time, said they did. But an equally important reason for the overestimate is that all survey studies more accurately represent some kinds of people than others, whereas population voting statistics are based on the entire population. That is, not everyone is easily found by survey interviewers, nor is everyone willing to be interviewed. Consider the problems of finding or of gaining interviews with migrant workers, the homeless, or people in illegal occupations such as prostitution or drug dealing. In addition, institutional populations such as those in jails, prisons, college dorms, convents, or the armed forces are not included in national survey samples. The same people who are hard for pollsters to locate and to interview also are those who are least apt to vote. Finally, many people don't like to admit that they skipped an election.

Still, even poll results show that a large number of Americans don't vote, even in presidential elections. Worse yet, the proportion voting in the 20th century has never approached the level recorded in the election of 1900. Keep in mind, however, that the 20th century saw major expansions in the types and numbers of people who were eligible to vote, and this no doubt affected the percentages of the eligible voters who actually voted. In 1900, in general, only males who were age 21 and above could vote. The 19th Amendment (1920) doubled this eligibility by giving women the right to vote. But women were not in the habit of voting, and so look at what happened to the voting participation curve in 1920 and 1924—it dropped drastically. It was not until the 1928 election that voting participation began to rise again. The 26th Amendment (1971) reduced the voting age to 18 nationally—the requirement had been 21 in all but a couple of states. The drop in voting participation in the 1972 election can be attributed partly to the fact that a new age group had been added to the eligible electorate and that this age group was not in the habit of voting.

➤ Data File: **HISTORY**
➤ Task: **Historical Trends**
➤ Variables: **12) VOTER PART**

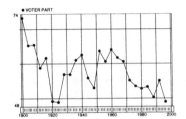

Percent of those eligible who voted for president

Not only have Americans become less likely to vote, there also are decided regional effects on voter turnouts.

➤ Data File: **STATES**
➤ Task: **Mapping**
➤ Variable 1: **97) %VOTED 96**
➤ View: **List: Rank**

RANK	CASE NAME	VALUE
1	Maine	71.90
2	Minnesota	64.07
3	Montana	62.06
4	South Dakota	60.53
5	Wyoming	59.43
6	Vermont	58.08
7	Iowa	57.72
8	Wisconsin	57.43
9	New Hampshire	57.30
10	Oregon	57.14

Maine had the highest percentage of voter turnout in the 1996 presidential election, with 71.9 percent. Minnesota (64.07 percent) and Montana (62.06 percent) were next highest. Nevada had the lowest percentage of voter turnout (38.31 percent).

Data File: **STATES**
Task: **Mapping**
Variable 1: **97) %VOTED 96**
➤ *Variable 2:* **8) THE SOUTH**
➤ *Views:* **Map**

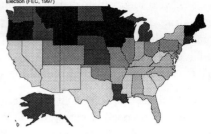

%VOTED 96 -- 1996: Percent of Voting Age Population who Voted in Presidential Election (FEC, 1997)

r = –0.476**

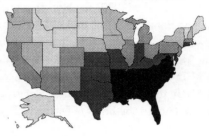

THE SOUTH -- Circulation of Southern Accents Magazine Per 100,000 (ABC)

Here we see that southern states had lower voter turnouts in the 1996 election, as indicated by the significant, negative correlation: –0.476**.

Data File: **STATES**
Task: **Mapping**
Variable 1: **97) %VOTED 96**
➤ *Variable 2:* **6) SUNBELT**
➤ *Views:* **Map**

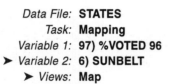

%VOTED 96 -- 1996: Percent of Voting Age Population who Voted in Presidential Election (FEC, 1997)

r = –0.676**

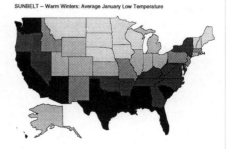

SUNBELT -- Warm Winters: Average January Low Temperature

In fact, however, low turnouts are typical in the Sunbelt states, which includes much of the South as well as some of the West. The correlation is stronger than with the South alone: –0.676**.

Part III: Government and the Individual

Voting turnout might also be affected by the demographic characteristics of states such as the degree of urbanism, education level, and income level.

Data File: **STATES**
Task: **Mapping**
Variable 1: **97) %VOTED 96**
➤ Variable 2: **4) URBAN USA**
➤ Views: **Map**

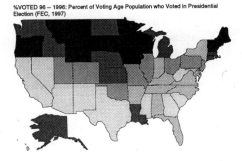

%VOTED 96 -- 1996: Percent of Voting Age Population who Voted in Presidential Election (FEC, 1997)

r = –0.419**

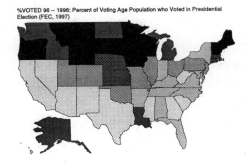

URBAN USA -- Percent of population that resides in a metropolitan statistical area 1996 (Census)

Here we see that there is a negative, statistically significant relationship (r= –0.419**) between urbanism and voter turnout. Thus, states that are less urban have higher rates of voter turnout.

Data File: **STATES**
Task: **Mapping**
Variable 1: **97) %VOTED 96**
➤ Variable 2: **126) %HIGH SCH**
➤ Views: **Map**

%VOTED 96 -- 1996: Percent of Voting Age Population who Voted in Presidential Election (FEC, 1997)

r = 0.559**

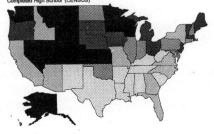

%HIGH SCH -- 1998: Percent of Population Age 25 and Older Who Have Completed High School (CENSUS)

Here we see that voter turnout is positively related to the percentage of the state's population that has a high school degree. The correlation coefficient r is 0.559 and it is statistically significant.

Data File: **STATES**
Task: **Mapping**
Variable 1: **97) %VOTED 96**
➤ Variable 2: **136) PER CAP$**
➤ Views: **Map**

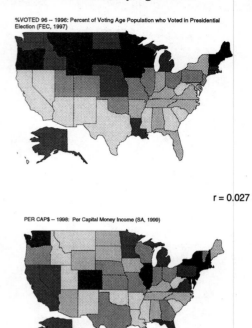

r = 0.027

Voter turnout is not, however, related to the per capita income of states. The correlation coefficient r is only 0.027 and it is not statistically significant.

Now let's turn to survey data to examine who is most likely to vote. Remember, however, that some of the people in surveys who say they voted did not actually vote. Nevertheless, these self-reports are sufficiently accurate to serve as a basis for analyzing who votes.

In general terms, we might expect that voting participation among citizens would vary according to demographic characteristics (e.g., education, age, income), political knowledge, and attitudes toward the workings of the political system (e.g., political trust). Let's begin with a demographic variable, education.

➤ Data File: **NES**
➤ Task: **Cross-tabulation**
➤ Row Variable: **1) VOTE?**
➤ Column Variable: **48) EDUCATION**
➤ View: **Table**
➤ Display: **Column %**

VOTE? by EDUCATION
Cramer's V: 0.324 **

		EDUCATION					
		Not HS Grd	HS Grad	Some Col	Coll.Grad.	Missing	TOTAL
VOTE?	Voted	77	244	256	323	5	900
		46.1%	63.2%	70.3%	91.5%		70.9%
	Did not	90	142	108	30	0	370
		53.9%	36.8%	29.7%	8.5%		29.1%
	Missing	2	0	2	2	0	6
	TOTAL	167	386	364	353	5	1270
		100.0%	100.0%	100.0%	100.0%		

When we examined the relationship between voter turnout and the education level of states, we found that states with had higher percentages of high school graduates had higher rates of voter turnout. Here the survey results confirm the link between education level and voting participation: The higher the education level of people, the more likely they are to vote. Note that 91.5 percent of those with a college degree said they had voted—which is almost twice as high as the voting turnout among those who didn't finish high school.

Data File: **NES**
Task: **Cross-tabulation**
Row Variable: **1) VOTE?**
➤ Column Variable: **46) REGION**
➤ View: **Table**
➤ Display: **Column %**

VOTE?   by   REGION
Cramer's V: 0.123 **

		REGION				
		East	West	Midwest	South	TOTAL
VOTE?	Voted	152	189	263	301	905
		72.4%	71.9%	78.5%	64.5%	71.0%
	Did not	58	74	72	166	370
		27.6%	28.1%	21.5%	35.5%	29.0%
	Missing	2	1	1	2	6
	TOTAL	210	263	335	467	1275
		100.0%	100.0%	100.0%	100.0%	

These findings also confirm those based on the 50 states: Southerners are the least likely to have voted.

Data File: **NES**
Task: **Cross-tabulation**
Row Variable: **1) VOTE?**
➤ Column Variable: **3) INTEREST?**
➤ View: **Table**
➤ Display: **Column %**

VOTE?   by   INTEREST?
Cramer's V: 0.193 **

		INTEREST?		
		Much	Lower	TOTAL
VOTE?	Voted	245	660	905
		87.5%	66.3%	71.0%
	Did not	35	335	370
		12.5%	33.7%	29.0%
	Missing	1	5	6
	TOTAL	280	995	1275
		100.0%	100.0%	

Not surprisingly, people rated as more interested in the campaign were more apt to have voted.

Data File: **NES**
Task: **Cross-tabulation**
Row Variable: **1) VOTE?**
➤ Column Variable: **5) INFORMED?**
➤ View: **Table**
➤ Display: **Column %**

VOTE?   by   INFORMED?
Cramer's V: 0.303 **

		INFORMED?		
		High	Aver/Low	TOTAL
VOTE?	Voted	425	480	905
		88.7%	60.3%	71.0%
	Did not	54	316	370
		11.3%	39.7%	29.0%
	Missing	3	3	6
	TOTAL	479	796	1275
		100.0%	100.0%	

And the more informed they were, the more apt people also were to have voted.

		Data File:	**NES**
		Task:	**Cross-tabulation**
		Row Variable:	**1) VOTE?**
	➤	Column Variable:	**99) MAKE DIFF**
	➤	View:	**Table**
	➤	Display:	**Column %**

VOTE?   by   MAKE DIFF
Cramer's V: 0.237 **

		MAKE DIFF				
		No differ	Neutral	Makes diff	Missing	TOTAL
VOTE?	Voted	80	111	710	4	901
		47.3%	62.4%	77.4%		71.3%
	Did not	89	67	207	7	363
		52.7%	37.6%	22.6%		28.7%
	Missing	1	1	4	0	6
	TOTAL	169	178	917	11	1264
		100.0%	100.0%	100.0%		

Here we see, as might be expected, that voting participation is higher among those who feel that having elections makes a difference in what happens.

Do patterns of voting make a difference in terms of policy? If certain types of people are less likely to vote, we might expect that their impact on public policy would be reduced. Let's examine differences between voters and nonvoters on the issue of abortion.

		Data File:	**NES**
		Task:	**Cross-tabulation**
	➤	Row Variable:	**59) ABORTION**
	➤	Column Variable:	**1) VOTE?**
	➤	View:	**Table**
	➤	Display:	**Column %**

ABORTION   by   VOTE?
Cramer's V: 0.121 **

		VOTE?			
		Voted	Did not	Missing	TOTAL
ABORTION	Never	86	67	2	153
		9.7%	18.4%		12.2%
	Sometimes	417	157	2	574
		47.0%	43.1%		45.8%
	Always	385	140	2	525
		43.4%	38.5%		41.9%
	Missing	17	6	0	23
	TOTAL	888	364	6	1252
		100.0%	100.0%		

Here there is a policy difference between voters and nonvoters: Voters are somewhat more likely to allow abortions than nonvoters are.

Your turn.

POLITICAL PARTIES

*No free country has ever been without political
parties, which are the offspring of Freedom.*
JAMES MADISON, 1787

Tasks: Mapping, Univariate, Cross-Tabulation, Scatterplot, Auto-Analyzer, Historical Trends
Data Files: NATIONS, GSS, NES, HISTORY

Political parties can be defined as organizations that sponsor candidates for political office and attempt (to a greater or lesser degree) to coordinate the actions of their elected members. Within this definition of party are three distinct groups of people, each with its important contribution.

First are the people who hold elective or appointive office or who run for office as candidates of the party. These can be identified as the *party-in-government*.

Second are the staff members and political activists who constitute the formal *party organization*. Included here are several million Americans who belong to political parties in the same way that people belong to other organizations: They contribute money, they attend meetings, and they may perform various duties such as passing out campaign literature or helping to turn out voters on election day.

Third, a party also includes all those members of the public who regard themselves as supporters of the party, and these people often are referred to as the *party-in-the-electorate*.

➤ *Data File:* **NATIONS**
➤ *Task:* **Mapping**
➤ *Variable 1:* **36) # PARTIES**
➤ *View:* **Map**

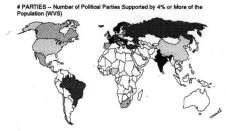

PARTIES -- Number of Political Parties Supported by 4% or More of the Population (WVS)

Nations differ a lot in their number of political parties. Some nations allow only one party and thus provide citizens with no political choices—one-party states are undemocratic and limit many freedoms people take for granted in democracies. In some nations there are two primary parties and any additional parties are too small to have any influence. But many nations have more than two major parties.

RANK	CASE NAME	VALUE
1	Slovenia	9
2	Belgium	8
3	Norway	7
3	France	7
3	Romania	7
6	India	6
6	Denmark	6
6	Hungary	6
6	Sweden	6
10	Brazil	5

Here we see that Slovenia has nine significant parties, defined as those able to attract at least 4 percent of the electorate (there are many additional smaller parties in Slovenia and elsewhere). Belgium has eight significant parties, while France, Norway, and Romania have seven each. At the bottom of the list, Ireland, Poland, and Japan have three parties, the United States and Nigeria have only two, and China allows only one.

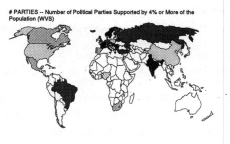

PARTIES -- Number of Political Parties Supported by 4% or More of the Population (WVS)

r = −0.467**

%BIG PARTY -- Percent of Support for the Largest Party (WVS)

This map shows the strength of the leading party. In each nation interviewers asked, "If there were a general election tomorrow, which party would you vote for?" Because some voters in each nation said they were undecided, only in Ireland did 50 percent support the same party. In Chile, 46 percent supported the same party, as did 45 percent of Americans. But in Slovenia and Belgium, the most popular party drew support from only 18 percent of the public and in Switzerland only 16 percent. Clearly, then, where there are many parties, each tends to be small, as is indicated by the negative correlation of −0.467**.

Nations not only differ in how many parties they have, they also differ in how easy it is to join a party. For example, in many nations (including Canada and Great Britain), parties are very tightly controlled national organizations and only candidates selected by the central party committees can run for office under the party label.

By comparison, American political parties are extremely easy to join. Even at the party-in-government level, people often run in and win party primaries without prior party participation and even in opposition to candidates backed by the party organization. For example, Dwight David Eisenhower successfully gained the Republican nomination for president in 1952, defeating Senator Robert A. Taft in primaries and in the convention, without any prior connections to the Republican Party. In fact, he had never even voted before (at that time, many military officers did not vote on the grounds that their allegiance was to the nation, not to any party). As for becoming an official member of the Republican or Democratic parties, it is pretty much a case of just showing up and joining. Even so, few Americans are actual party members (recall how few give money to a party). For most people, political parties are labels attached to candidates and political positions, and their own party "membership" is really only a preference or self-identification.

➤ *Data File:* **GSS**
➤ *Task:* **Univariate**
➤ *Primary Variable:* **62) POL.PARTY**
➤ *View:* **Pie**

POL.PARTY -- Generally speaking, do you usually think of yourself as a Republican, Democrat, Independent, or what?

		Freq.	%
■	1) Democrat	1316	47.7
▨	2) Independ.	477	17.3
■	3) Republican	967	35.0
	TOTAL (N)	2760	100.0
	Missing	72	

Most Americans are partisans, either Democrats or Republicans, but nearly one in five Americans calls themselves a political independent. Those naming a third party fall below 1 percent.

Partisanship influences a number of other attitudes and activities. Partisanship has a strong effect on the candidates that people support.

➤ *Data File:* **NES**
➤ *Task:* **Cross-tabulation**
➤ *Row Variable:* **2) PRES IN 96**
➤ *Column Variable:* **43) POL.PARTY**
➤ *View:* **Table**
➤ *Display:* **Column %**

PRES IN 96   by   POL.PARTY
Cramer's V: 0.540 **

		POL.PARTY				
		Democrat	Independ.	Republican	Missing	TOTAL
PRES IN 96	Clinton	319	97	28	28	444
		90.9%	45.1%	11.3%		54.5%
	Dole	12	55	189	19	256
		3.4%	25.6%	76.2%		31.4%
	Perot	20	63	31	9	114
		5.7%	29.3%	12.5%		14.0%
	Missing	127	125	88	71	411
	TOTAL	351	215	248	127	814
		100.0%	100.0%	100.0%		

This table clearly shows the strong influence partisanship had on voters' choices in the 1996 presidential election. Ninety-one percent of the Democrats voted to reelect President Clinton. Seventy-six percent of Republicans voted for Robert Dole. Thus, part of the reason Senator Dole lost the 1996 presidential election is that he did not retain as much support from his own party as President Clinton did. Dole also did not gain as much support from independent voters. Independents were most likely to support Clinton in 1996.

The exit polls conducted by the media during the 2000 presidential election show similar results. Ninety-one percent of Republican voters cast their ballots for George W. Bush while 86 percent of Democrats supported Al Gore. George W. Bush held a slight lead among independent voters, receiving the support of 47 percent of the independents compared to the 45 percent who cast their ballots for Al Gore.

While partisanship clearly is linked to voters' choices in presidential elections, partisanship is not always as strongly linked to other political attitudes. Let's examine the relationship between partisanship and political ideology.

Data File: **NES**
Task: **Cross-tabulation**
➤ Row Variable: **4) IDEOLOGY**
➤ Column Variable: **43) POL.PARTY**
➤ View: **Table**
➤ Display: **Column %**

IDEOLOGY   by   POL.PARTY
Cramer's V: 0.346 **

	POL.PARTY				
IDEOLOGY	Democrat	Independ.	Republican	Missing	TOTAL
Liberal	143	63	20	22	226
	39.1%	22.6%	6.8%		24.0%
Moderate	145	133	59	34	337
	39.6%	47.7%	19.9%		35.8%
Conserv.	78	83	217	21	378
	21.3%	29.7%	73.3%		40.2%
Missing	112	61	40	50	263
TOTAL	366	279	296	127	941
	100.0%	100.0%	100.0%		

Republicans show the greatest consistency in their ideology. Nearly three out of four Republicans call themselves conservatives. The Democratic party is much more diverse in terms of ideology. Democrats are almost evenly split between liberals and moderates. Furthermore, one in five Democrats considers themselves to be conservative.

The Democratic and Republican party organizations rely on individual American citizens to contribute money to support their activities. In the exercise on political participation, we saw that only 5 percent of Americans contribute money to a political party. Are partisans more willing to contribute money than independents?

Data File: **NES**
Task: **Cross-tabulation**
➤ Row Variable: **19) PARTY $**
➤ Column Variable: **43) POL PARTY**
➤ View: **Table**
➤ Display: **Column %**

PARTY $ by   POL.PARTY
Cramer's V: 0.068

	POL.PARTY				
PARTY $	Democrat	Independ.	Republican	Missing	TOTAL
Yes	24	11	24	4	59
	5.0%	3.2%	7.1%		5.1%
No	454	329	312	122	1095
	95.0%	96.8%	92.9%		94.9%
Missing	0	0	0	1	1
TOTAL	478	340	336	127	1154
	100.0%	100.0%	100.0%		

Republicans and Democrats are slightly more likely to contribute money to the political parties than are independents, but the percentages for all groups are very small and quite similar. As a result, the differences in this table do not meet the criteria for statistical significance, and we cannot be certain that even such small differences exist among the American public. Contributing to the political parties is a very infrequent task for all U.S. citizens.

Your turn.

WORKSHEET

NAME:

COURSE:

DATE:

EXERCISE
9

REVIEW QUESTIONS

Based on the first part of this exercise, answer True or False to the following items:

Most democratic nations have at least three major political parties.	T	F
Most Democrats say they are liberals.	T	F
Nearly one-half of the American electorate considers themselves to be political independents.	T	F
In the 1996 and 2000 presidential elections, at least three-fourths of partisans supported their own party's presidential candidate.	T	F
Partisans are considerably more likely than independents to have contributed money to a political party.	T	F

EXPLORIT QUESTIONS

1. In the opening section of this exercise, we noted that American political parties are often discussed in terms of three components: the party in government, the party in the electorate, and the party organization. Beginning with the party-in-government component, one can note that two major parties, the Democrats and the Republicans, have dominated the government over the past century. All other parties are referred to as third parties or minor parties. How many third-party candidates have been a part of the government? Let's investigate by looking at the percentage of seats in the U.S. House and Senate controlled by members of a third party or by political independents.

> ➤ Data File: **HISTORY**
> ➤ Task: **Historical Trends**
> ➤ Variables: **68) HSE-OTH**
> **69) SEN-OTH**

Answer True or False to the following items:

The percentage of third-party members in the U.S. House often exceeds 20 percent. (Hint: Look at the scale on the left-hand side of the graph. The numbers listed are the percentages of seats held by third parties.)	T	F
The percentage of third-party members in the U.S. House and Senate has increased substantially in recent years.	T	F

Exercise 9: Political Parties

145

2. Now let's compare the percentage of seats held by the Democratic versus the Republican party in the U.S. House. The party that has the most seats is referred to as the majority party. The majority party leader becomes the Speaker of the House, and the majority party controls the chairs of all of the congressional committees. The majority party has considerable influence over the decisions made by Congress.

> *Data File:* **HISTORY**
> *Task:* **Historical Trends**
> ➤ *Variables:* **16) %DEM HOUSE**
> **70) %REP HOUSE**

Answer True or False to the following items:

The Democratic party was the majority party in the U.S. House from the middle of the 1950s to the middle of the 1990s.   T   F

Throughout the 20th century, the Democratic party was more likely to be the majority party in the House than was the Republican party.   T   F

3. Now let's look at the party in the electorate. Earlier we saw that partisans were no more likely than independents to contribute money to political candidates. Are partisans more likely than independents to participate in other types of political activities?

Fill in the table at the end of this question after completing each of the following analyses:

> ➤ *Data File:* **NES**
> ➤ *Task:* **Cross-tabulation**
> ➤ *Row Variable:* **1) VOTE?**
> ➤ *Column Variable:* **43) POL.PARTY**
> ➤ *View:* **Table**
> ➤ *Display:* **Column %**

> ➤ *Row Variable:* **39) VOTED 98?**
> ➤ *Column Variable:* **43) POL.PARTY**
> ➤ *View:* **Table**
> ➤ *Display:* **Column %**

> ➤ *Row Variable:* **5) INFORMED?**
> ➤ *Column Variable:* **43) POL.PARTY**
> ➤ *View:* **Table**
> ➤ *Display:* **Column %**

(Note: V for each of these tables is statistically significant.)

NES SURVEY

	DEMOCRAT	INDEPEND.	REPUBLICAN
1) VOTE? % who voted	_____ %	_____ %	_____ %
39) VOTED 98? % who voted	_____ %	_____ %	_____ %
5) INFORMED? % who were highly informed	_____ %	_____ %	_____ %

Answer True or False to the following items:

Democrats and Republicans are about equally likely to vote, but independents
are considerably less likely to vote.   T   F

Those who claim a party preference are generally less informed about politics
than are independents.   T   F

4.   "Because of their keen interest in following politics, independents make their decisions on an issue-
by-issue basis and refuse to be categorized by party." Do you agree or disagree with this statement?
Why or why not? Use the information you collected in Question 3 to support your position.

5.   In Exercise 8, low voter turnouts in the United States were attributed, at least in part, to the limited
choices posed by the two-party system. Let's look at other nations to see if there is any support for
this idea.

> ➤ *Data File:* **NATIONS**
> ➤ *Task:* **Scatterplot**
> ➤ *Dependent Variable:* **38) % VOTED**
> ➤ *Independent Variable:* **36) # PARTIES**
> ➤ *View:* **Reg. Line**

Answer True or False to the following items:

The greater the number of political parties in a nation, the higher the percentage voting.   T   F

This scatterplot supports the idea that the limited choice of parties in the United States may be depressing the voter turnout rate.   T   F

6. Let's use the AUTO-ANALYZER task to see who's most likely to be a Democrat and who's most likely to be a Republican.

> ➤ Data File: **GSS**
> ➤ Task: **Auto-Analyzer**
> ➤ Variable: **60) DEM/REP**
> ➤ View: **Univariate**

For each demographic variable listed below, indicate whether there is any significant effect. If so, indicate which category is most likely and which is least likely to identify with the Democratic Party.

	IS THE EFFECT SIGNIFICANT?		CATEGORY MOST LIKELY TO BE DEMOCRAT	CATEGORY LEAST LIKELY TO BE DEMOCRAT
View: **Sex**	Yes	No	_____	_____
View: **Race**	Yes	No	_____	_____
View: **Religion**	Yes	No	_____	_____
View: **Region**	Yes	No	_____	_____
View: **Education**	Yes	No	_____	_____
View: **Income**	Yes	No	_____	_____

7. Based on the results in Question 6, describe the characteristics of those who are most likely to be Democrats.

Based on the results in Question 6, describe the characteristics of those who are least likely to be Democrats.

8. Finally, let's examine the financial standing of the two major parties. An important component of the party organization is the ability to raise money. Money is needed to fund the national headquarters, to pay staff, to conduct polling, and to assist the party's candidates. Are the two political parties on an equal financial footing? Let's examine the money raised (in millions of dollars) by the Democratic and Republican parties over recent decades.

> ➤ *Data File:* **HISTORY**
>   ➤ *Task:* **Historical Trends**
> ➤ *Variables:* **71) DEM$**
>   **72) REP$**

As you can see from the graph, the Republican party has consistently raised more money than the Democratic party in recent decades. Why do you think that the Republican party is able to raise more money?

ELECTIONS

Bad politicians are sent to Washington by good people who don't vote.

WILLIAM E. SIMON, 1985

Tasks: Mapping
Data Files: STATES

By law, all positions in the House of Representatives and one-third of those in the Senate are filled by an election held on the first Tuesday after the first Monday in November in every even-numbered year. Consequently, all members of the House face reelection every two years and all senators every six. In addition, every second national election is a presidential election as presidents of the United States serve a four-year term (and are limited to two elected terms by the 22nd Amendment, adopted in 1951). Unlike elections for other offices, both national and local, American presidents are elected in a somewhat unusual way.

➤ *Data File:* **STATES**
➤ *Task:* **Mapping**
➤ *Variable 1:* **178) GORE**
➤ *View:* **Map**

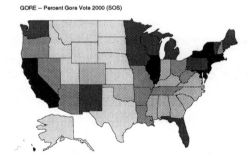

GORE -- Percent Gore Vote 2000 (SOS)

The darker the state, the higher the percentage of the vote won by Al Gore. Since these are the votes cast by individual voters, they are referred to as the **popular** vote. Combining all the votes cast nationwide in 2000, Al Gore won the popular vote, receiving approximately 500,000 more votes than George W. Bush. However, 105 million votes were cast in the 2000 presidential election, so Gore's margin of victory over Bush in the popular vote was less than 1 percent of the total votes cast. The popular vote in the 2000 presidential election was one of the closest in history. Despite winning the popular vote, Gore lost the presidential election to Bush. Let's see how this happened.

Data File: **STATES**

Task: **Mapping**

➤ Variable 1: **185) STATES '00**

➤ View: **Map**

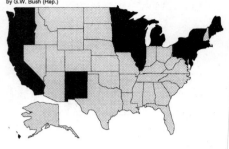

STATES '00 -- -- 2000: Dark States Carried by Gore (Dem.), Light States Carried by G.W. Bush (Rep.)

Gore had the most votes in 20 states plus Washington D.C. George W. Bush won 30 states. Bush garnered 271 electoral college votes from those 30 states. A candidate needs to win a majority of the electoral college votes to become president. Since there are 538 electoral college votes, a candidate needs to win a minimum of 270 electoral college votes to become president. George W. Bush won the presidency with only one more electoral college vote than needed. The 2000 presidential election was indeed an extremely close race.

Electoral votes exist because the Constitution does not provide for the direct election of the president or vice president. Instead, Article II of the Constitution directs that the president and vice president shall be elected by a group known as the **electoral college**:

> Each State shall appoint, in such Manner as the Legislature thereof may direct, a Number of Electors, equal to the whole Number of Senators and Representatives to which the State may be entitled in the Congress; but no Senator or Representative, or Person holding an Office of Trust or Profit under the United States, shall be appointed an Elector.

Once appointed, each state's electors were directed to gather (thereby constituting an electoral college) whereupon each would vote for two persons—at least one of whom could not be a resident of their state—and these votes then were to be forwarded to the president of the Senate (who always is the current vice president). The votes of all electors from all states then were to be opened and counted.

The person receiving a majority of the electoral college votes was elected president. After the president was elected, the person receiving the second most votes was elected vice president. When no person received a majority, or a tie occurred, then the House of Representatives chose the president from the five highest vote getters in the electoral college. The representatives of each state voted as a state delegation and thus had one vote. The person having the majority of the votes was elected president. If there was a tie for vice president, the Senate elected the vice president. Each senator cast a vote, and it required a majority to be elected.

In 1804 the 12th Amendment made several changes in this procedure. Each elector was to cast two separate votes, one for president, the other for vice president. When no person received a majority, or a tie occurred, in the vote for president, then the House of Representatives chose the president from the three highest vote getters in the electoral college. Again, the representatives of each state voted as a state delegation and thus had one vote. The person having the majority of the votes was elected president. When no person received the majority, or a tie occurred, in the vote for vice president, the Senate elected the vice president from the top two vote getters in the electoral college. Each senator cast a vote, and it required a majority to be elected.

Because each state has the number of electors equal to its total membership in Congress, and each state is guaranteed at least one representative and two senators, no state will have fewer than three electors. The 23rd Amendment to the Constitution, which took effect in 1961, gives three electoral college votes to the residents of Washington D.C. Since the nation's capital is not part of any state, prior to that date, residents of Washington D.C. had no say in the selection of the president. The Constitution leaves it to the states *how* the electors shall be selected, and in early days they often were selected by the state legislatures. As time passed, and political parties emerged, people began to campaign to be selected as electors on the basis of their promise to vote for a specific presidential candidate. Eventually, electors were selected by the voters in each state.

Thus, we do not vote directly for the president or vice president. Instead, each party files a slate of electors committed to cast their votes (now called electoral votes) for the party's presidential and vice presidential candidates. When we mark our ballots for a particular person for president, what we really are doing is voting for the appropriate slate of electors. The winning candidate in each state, the one with the most votes whether or not these are more than half of all votes, receives *all* of that state's electoral votes because the winner's slate of electors is elected. Following each election, in December, each elector casts his or her official vote, and these are sent to the U.S. Senate where they are counted under the supervision of the vice president (of the previous administration) and reported to Congress. Once in a while an elector votes for someone other than the candidate he or she was pledged to support. In 2000, one of the electors chosen from Washington D.C. left the ballot blank, reducing Al Gore's electoral college vote from 267 to 266. The elector left the ballot blank to protest the fact that residents of Washington D.C. have no voting members in the U.S. Congress.

Although it takes a majority of electoral votes to be elected, at the state level it's winner-take-all. All of a state's electoral votes go to the candidate receiving the most votes. Maine and Nebraska use winner-take-all at the state level to assign two of their electors and winner-take-all at the congressional district to assign their remaining electors. Sometimes, candidates win a state's electors with less than a majority vote. In fact, a candidate only needs to win more votes than any other candidate on the ballot. This is winning by a **plurality** of the votes cast. Typically in U.S. presidential elections, almost all of the votes are cast for the Democratic or Republican presidential candidate. However, when a significant portion of the vote is cast for a third-party or independent candidate, a presidential candidate may win many of the electoral college votes by plurality victories in the states' popular vote. When this occurs in a number of states, the candidate winning the electoral college may have a plurality of the popular vote but not a majority of the popular vote. Presidents who receive less than half of the total popular vote are sometimes called "minority presidents." President Clinton won less than a majority of the popular vote in the 1992 and 1996 presidential elections due to the number of votes cast for third-party candidate Ross Perot.

      Data File: **STATES**
         Task: **Mapping**
➤ Variable 1: **84) ELECTOR90**
       ➤ View: **List: Rank**

RANK	CASE NAME	VALUE
1	California	54
2	New York	33
3	Texas	32
4	Florida	25
5	Pennsylvania	23
6	Illinois	22
7	Ohio	21
8	Michigan	18
9	New Jersey	15
10	North Carolina	14

Here we see the current distribution of electoral votes by state in 2000. California has 54 electoral votes, or 10 percent of the total. Next come New York (33), Texas (32), Florida (25), Pennsylvania (23), Illinois (22), and Ohio (21). In contrast, seven states have only 3 electoral votes and six have only 4. Put another way, the 13 least populous states have fewer electoral votes (45) among them than does California alone.

Every ten years, following each census, the House of Representatives is **reapportioned** as seats in the House are shifted to growing states. Reapportionment of the House automatically shifts electoral votes too. Consequently, the number of electoral votes shifts in response to shifts in the relative size of state populations.

Electoral college vote totals will change for some states by the 2004 presidential election. Results from the 2000 census show which states have gained more citizens and which states have lost citizens, or at least not have grown as fast. The 2000 census figures are used to reapportion the seats in the House of Representatives and thus adjust the electoral college votes for each state as well.

Data File: **STATES**
Task: **Mapping**
➤ *Variable 1:* **191) EC GAIN00**
➤ *View:* **Map**

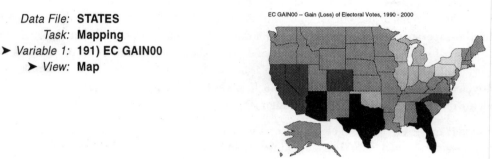

EC GAIN00 -- Gain (Loss) of Electoral Votes, 1990 - 2000

Two states, New York and Pennsylvania, will have two fewer electoral college votes in 2004 than they did in the 2000 presidential election. Eight other states, mostly in the Midwest, will lose one electoral college vote. On the other hand, four states—Arizona, Florida, Georgia, and Texas—will gain two electoral college votes, while four additional states will pick up one vote each. Once again the movement of Americans away from the "rust belt" of the Midwest and East to the Sunbelt of the South and West will alter the political clout of the states in presidential elections.

Your turn.

EXERCISE 11

INTEREST GROUPS AND PACS

Politics has got so expensive that it takes a lot of money to even get beat.

WILL ROGERS, 1931

Tasks: Mapping, Univariate, Cross-Tabulation
Data Files: NATIONS, GSS, HOUSE106

Quite often in politics elected public officials or candidates for political office attack "special interest groups" or "pressure groups," or they suggest that their opponents or critics are in league with such groups. What is the difference between a "special interest group," an "interest group," a "pressure group," and a "group of public-spirited citizens"? The answer a person gives to this question might very well depend on which side of an issue the person favors. People tend to view groups on the other side of an issue in negative terms, referring to them as "special interest groups" or "pressure groups." On the other hand, groups involved in political issues often tend to view themselves as citizens who are looking out for the public interest either directly or indirectly.

Here we will use the term "interest group" in a neutral fashion to refer to any group of people who share some political value and attempt to pursue that value in the political system. This shared political value might be economic (e.g., views on tax decreases, aid to education, minimum wage laws) or noneconomic (e.g., views on abortion, freedom of speech, the rights of defendants in court).

Two basic kinds of interest groups exist: *affinity groups*, which are unorganized publics sharing a particular condition or concern such as elderly people who feel that current Social Security payments are inadequate, and *organized groups* (such as the American Association of Retired Persons), which collect dues and use them to sustain professional staffs to influence both public opinion and public officials. Another example of an affinity group consists of people who share certain views about civil liberties. Not everyone who shares this set of views is part of an organized group, but an example of an organized group dealing with civil liberties is the American Civil Liberties Union.

If you think about affinity groups, you will recognize that most, if not all, Americans belong to an interest group and most of us belong to many. The problem is that we tend to define *our* interest groups as unselfish and in the general interest while opposing *other* people's interest groups as selfish and out to harm the rest of us.

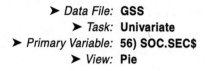

> ➤ *Data File:* **GSS**
> ➤ *Task:* **Univariate**
> ➤ *Primary Variable:* **56) SOC.SEC$**
> ➤ *View:* **Pie**

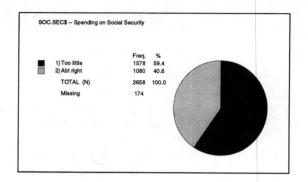

SOC.SEC$ -- Spending on Social Security

	Freq.	%
■ 1) Too little	1578	59.4
▨ 2) Abt right	1080	40.6
TOTAL (N)	2658	100.0
Missing	174	

Here we see that over half (59.4 percent) of Americans think we are spending too little on Social Security. There can be little doubt that among those wanting an increase is an interest group that has become a favorite in political campaigning, variously referred to as "our neglected senior citizens" or as the "selfish Social Security lobby," depending on the candidate.

> *Data File:* **GSS**
> ➤ *Task:* **Cross-tabulation**
> ➤ *Row Variable:* **56) SOC.SEC$**
> ➤ *Column Variable:* **66) AGE**
> ➤ *View:* **Table**
> ➤ *Display:* **Column %**

SOC.SEC$ by   AGE
Cramer's V: 0.105 **

		AGE						
		Under 30	30-39	40-49	50-64	65 & Over	Missing	TOTAL
S O C . S E C $	Too little	294	400	349	313	221	1	1577
		60.0%	63.4%	62.4%	60.4%	48.5%		59.4%
	Abt right	196	231	210	205	235	3	1077
		40.0%	36.6%	37.6%	39.6%	51.5%		40.6%
	Missing	47	56	21	27	23	0	174
	TOTAL	490	631	559	518	456	4	2654
		100.0%	100.0%	100.0%	100.0%	100.0%		

Everyone knows that people on Social Security are militant about their rights and never think they are getting enough benefits. But in this case, what "everyone" knows, isn't so. People over 65 are least likely to think too little is being spent on Social Security.

> *Data File:* **GSS**
> *Task:* **Cross-tabulation**
> ➤ *Row Variable:* **29) GUN LAW?**
> ➤ *Column Variable:* **13) OWN GUN?**
> ➤ *View:* **Table**
> ➤ *Display:* **Column %**

GUN LAW?   by   OWN GUN?
Cramer's V: 0.243 **

		OWN GUN?			
		Yes	No	Missing	TOTAL
G U N L A W ?	Favor	460	1067	8	1527
		71.4%	90.3%		83.6%
	Oppose	184	115	3	299
		28.6%	9.7%		16.4%
	Missing	10	33	952	995
	TOTAL	644	1182	963	1826
		100.0%	100.0%		

Something else we all know is that gun owners bitterly oppose all gun control legislation. But this table shows that isn't so. Here we see that over 70% of gun owners favored a law requiring that a person obtain a police permit before buying a gun. It's not gun owners as an affinity interest group who oppose gun control laws; rather, it is the organized interest group known as the National Rifle Association that "speaks on behalf of gun owners" in opposition to such laws.

These findings let us recognize something very important about interest groups—that organized interest groups may or may not represent the constituency for whom they claim to speak.

Data File: **GSS**
Task: **Cross-tabulation**
Row Variable: **29) GUN LAW?**
➤ Column Variable: **56) SOC.SEC$**
➤ View: **Table**
➤ Display: **Column %**

GUN LAW?   by   SOC.SEC$
Cramer's V: 0.005

		SOC.SEC$			
		Too little	Abt right	Missing	TOTAL
GUN LAW?	Favor	844	603	88	1447
		83.2%	83.5%		83.3%
	Oppose	171	119	12	290
		16.8%	16.5%		16.7%
	Missing	563	358	74	995
	TOTAL	1015	722	174	1737
		100.0%	100.0%		

An extremely important point about memberships in interest groups is that the same person is usually included in a variety of such groups. Thus, a person might side with particular people on one issue and different people on another issue. Here we see that the views of people on Social Security spending are not at all related to their views on gun control. Thus, the group of people who favor gun control could be a very different mix of people than the group of people who favor greater spending on Social Security.

This is important for the stability of a political system because it means that there are not just two permanent "sides" in political conflict. The coalitions for or against something can shift with the issue. A person who loses on one issue might win on another issue. This helps to reduce the overall conflict within society.

➤ Data File: **NATIONS**
➤ Task: **Mapping**
➤ Variable 1: **7) INTEREST G**
➤ View: **List: Rank**

RANK	CASE NAME	VALUE
1	Iceland	27
2	Netherlands	24
2	Norway	24
4	Latvia	23
4	United States	23
4	Finland	23
7	South Korea	20
8	Switzerland	18
8	Austria	18
8	Brazil	18

Organized interest groups are not peculiar to American politics. About 1 person in 4 belongs to an organized political interest group in Iceland, the Netherlands, Norway, the United States, Finland, and Latvia. That drops to 1 in 20 persons in Argentina, Spain, and Romania, and to only 1 in 33 in Japan.

We noted earlier that organized interest groups may or may not accurately reflect the concerns and preferences of those they presume to represent. But, if this is so, why do politicians pay so much attention to organized interest groups? Because they are the primary source of campaign funds.

A primary fact of life facing every elected official is that the next election is always just around the corner and it costs money to win elections. Since they are up for reelection every two years, many members of the House are never really able to cease campaigning, and perhaps the single most central aspect of campaigning is fund-raising.

> ➤ *Data File:* **HOUSE106**
> ➤ *Task:* **Univariate**
> ➤ *Primary Variable:* **21) CAMPAIGN $**
> ➤ *View:* **Pie**

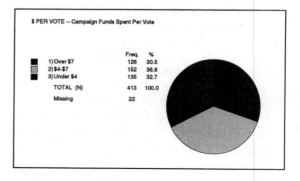

CAMPAIGN $ -- Net campaign expenditures from Jan. 1, 1997 through Dec. 31, 1998. The lowest third of the candidates spent between $39,786 and $366,864. Middle third = $370,757 to $686,929. Highest third = $692,259 to $3,147,256.

		Freq.	%
■	1) Lowest 3rd	146	33.7
▨	2) Middle 3rd	143	33.0
■	3) Highest 3r	144	33.3
	TOTAL (N)	433	100.0
	Missing	2	

More than two-thirds of the representatives spent at least $370,000 on their 1998 campaigns. The highest amount ($7,323,738) was spent by former House Speaker Newt Gingrich (Republican from Georgia). However, Gingrich resigned his seat at the beginning of the 106th Congress and is not included in the HOUSE106 data file; his replacement (Isakson) is included instead. Excluding Gingrich, the representative who spent the most was Richard Gephardt (Democrat from Missouri), who spent $3,147,256. At the other end, Gregory Meeks (Democrat from New York) spent only $39,786, and Mark Sanford (Republican from South Carolina) spent only $49,150. Excluding Gingrich, the average amount spent by representatives in their 1998 campaigns was over $600,000.

> *Data File:* **HOUSE106**
> *Task:* **Univariate**
> ➤ *Primary Variable:* **22) $ PER VOTE**
> ➤ *View:* **Pie**

$ PER VOTE -- Campaign Funds Spent Per Vote

		Freq.	%
■	1) Over $7	126	30.5
▨	2) $4-$7	152	36.8
■	3) Under $4	135	32.7
	TOTAL (N)	413	100.0
	Missing	22	

Another way to examine campaign spending is on the basis of the amount spent for each vote the candidate received. More than 125 representatives each spent more than $7 per vote. Now let's see where all of this money comes from.

Data File: **HOUSE106**
Task: **Univariate**
➤ Primary Variable: **20) %PAC CONTR**
➤ View: **Pie**

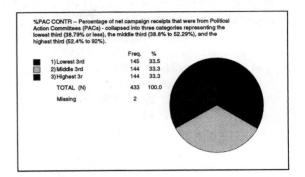

Much of the campaign money came from political action committees—PACs. Almost any organization—a corporation, a union, a professional association, a neighborhood club, or even a bowling team—can create its own PAC and then raise funds from member contributions or even by seeking funds from nonmembers. Over a third of the members of the House received more than half of their total funding from PACs. The primary purpose of political action committees is to get around laws limiting campaign contributions. Why does so much money come from PACs? One reason is that PACs can contribute $5,000 to a candidate while an individual can contribute only $1,000. Second, there are over 4,600 PACs.

Data File: **HOUSE106**
➤ Task: **Cross-tabulation**
➤ Row Variable: **21) CAMPAIGN $**
➤ Column Variable: **9) PARTY**
➤ View: **Table**
➤ Display: **Column %**

CAMPAIGN $ by PARTY
Cramer's V: 0.080

		PARTY			
		Democrat	Republican	Missing	TOTAL
CAMPAIGN $	Lowest 3rd	79	67	0	146
		37.4%	30.3%		33.8%
	Middle 3rd	68	74	1	142
		32.2%	33.5%		32.9%
	Highest 3r	64	80	0	144
		30.3%	36.2%		33.3%
	Missing	0	2	0	2
	TOTAL	211	221	1	432
		100.0%	100.0%		

Since we know from Exercise 9 that higher-income people tend to prefer the Republican Party, we should expect that Republican candidates have an easier time raising money. Here we see that while Republicans are more likely to raise large sums of money than Democrats, the difference is not statistically significant.

Data File: **HOUSE106**
Task: **Cross-tabulation**
➤ Row Variable: **22) $ PER VOTE**
➤ Column Variable: **9) PARTY**
➤ View: **Table**
➤ Display: **Column %**

$ PER VOTE by PARTY
Cramer's V: 0.084

		PARTY			
		Democrat	Republican	Missing	TOTAL
$ PER VOTE	Over $7	65	61	0	126
		31.7%	29.5%		30.6%
	$4-$7	67	84	1	151
		32.7%	40.6%		36.7%
	Under $4	73	62	0	135
		35.6%	30.0%		32.8%
	Missing	6	16	0	22
	TOTAL	205	207	1	412
		100.0%	100.0%		

Here we see that Republicans and Democrats spent equally on votes during their campaigns.

Data File: **HOUSE106**
Task: **Cross-tabulation**
➤ Row Variable: **20) %PAC CONTR**
➤ Column Variable: **9) PARTY**
➤ View: **Table**
➤ Display: **Column %**

%PAC CONTR   by   PARTY
Cramer's V: 0.263 **

		PARTY			
		Democrat	Republican	Missing	TOTAL
%PAC CONTR	Lowest 3rd	51	93	1	144
		24.2%	42.1%		33.3%
	Middle 3rd	64	80	0	144
		30.3%	36.2%		33.3%
	Highest 3r	96	48	0	144
		45.5%	21.7%		33.3%
	Missing	0	2	0	2
	TOTAL	211	221	1	432
		100.0%	100.0%		

Here is a significant difference. Democrats tend to receive a far larger proportion of their campaign funds from political action committees (PACs) than do Republicans.

Data File: **HOUSE106**
Task: **Cross-tabulation**
Row Variable: **20) %PAC CONTR**
➤ Column Variable: **12) # TERMS**
➤ View: **Table**
➤ Display: **Column %**

%PAC CONTR   by   # TERMS
Cramer's V: 0.261 **

		# TERMS			
		One	2-4 terms	5 or more	TOTAL
%PAC CONTR	Lowest 3rd	30	78	37	145
		76.9%	35.5%	21.3%	33.5%
	Middle 3rd	8	83	53	144
		20.5%	37.7%	30.5%	33.3%
	Highest 3r	1	59	84	144
		2.6%	26.8%	48.3%	33.3%
	Missing	2	0	0	2
	TOTAL	39	220	174	433
		100.0%	100.0%	100.0%	

To whom do PACs give their money? Obviously, they usually want to focus their money on candidates who agree with their policy positions. But, given a limited amount of money, PACs must still attempt to disperse their money in such a way that it is not wasted. One way to do this is give money to candidates who are most likely to win and give little or no money to candidates who are likely to lose. These results show that the more terms a representative has served, the higher is the percentage of campaign money that came from PACs. Almost half of those representatives who had served five or more terms were in the highest third in terms of percentage of their campaign money coming from PACs. On the other end, most first-term representatives were in the lowest third in terms of the percentage of their campaign money coming from PACs.

Your turn.

WORKSHEET

NAME:

COURSE:

DATE:

EXERCISE

11

REVIEW QUESTIONS

Based on the first part of this exercise, answer True or False to the following items:

Most gun owners oppose gun control legislation.	T	F
Only a small minority of Americans belong to an affinity interest group.	T	F
Organized interest groups exist in only a few countries.	T	F
The stability of the American political system is aided by the fact that there are no permanent "sides" in political conflict—the coalition for or against something can shift with the particular issue involved.	T	F
Republican representatives spent a much greater amount on their campaigns than Democratic representatives did.	T	F
Democratic representatives received a larger proportion of their campaign funds from PACs than Republican representatives did.	T	F
Representatives who have served more terms received a higher proportion of their campaign funds from PACs.	T	F

EXPLORIT QUESTIONS

1. As indicated before, older people constitute an affinity group. During the 2000 election campaign, both major party candidates made appeals to the elderly on the basis of Social Security issues and medical care issues. However, in the first part of this exercise, we found that contrary to what we might assume, a majority of those over 65 didn't think increases in Social Security were needed. Let's now see whether older people were more likely to want the government to help with medical costs.

    > *Data File:* **GSS**
    > *Task:* **Cross-tabulation**
    > *Row Variable:* **79) GOV.MED.**
    > *Column Variable:* **66) AGE**
    > *View:* **Table**
    > *Display:* **Column %**

Make sure to read the variable description for GOV.MED. and then answer True or False to the following items.

People 65 and older were the ones who most favored government help
with medical costs.   T   F

The younger people are, the more likely they are to favor government help
with medical costs.   T   F

2.   Let's examine some other affinity groups, starting with the residents of big cities.

> Data File: **GSS**
> Task: **Cross-tabulation**
> ➤ Row Variable: **57) BIG CITY$**
> ➤ Column Variable: **55) URBAN?**
> ➤ View: **Table**
> ➤ Display: **Column %**

The majority of big-city residents think the government is spending too little on the
problems of big cities.   T   F

Pretty much everyone thinks too little is being spent on big-city problems, regardless
of where they live.   T   F

3.   African Americans form an affinity group.

> Data File: **GSS**
> Task: **Cross-tabulation**
> ➤ Row Variable: **58) BLACK$**
> ➤ Column Variable: **3) WH/AFR.AM**
> ➤ View: **Table**
> ➤ Display: **Column %**

Most African Americans think too little is being spent on improving the conditions
of Blacks.   T   F

4.   There are various kinds of religious-political groups that constitute both affinity groups (e.g., those
who believe in prayer in public schools versus those who don't) and organized groups (the Christian
Coalition, People for the American Way, Bread for the World, American Jewish Committee, etc.).
Let's see whether views on prayer and Bible reading in the public schools are affected by how religious people consider themselves to be.

> Data File: **GSS**
> Task: **Cross-tabulation**
> ➤ Row Variable: **7) SCH.PRAYER**
> ➤ Column Variable: **99) RELPERSN**
> ➤ View: **Table**
> ➤ Display: **Column %**

People who consider themselves to be very religious are the ones who most
support prayer in public schools. T F

A majority of those who are not at all religious oppose prayer in public schools. T F

5. Those elected to Congress often represent affinity groups within their district. Let's look at the
    racial/ethnic composition of congressional districts.

> ➤ *Data File:* **HOUSE106**
> ➤ *Task:* **Univariate**
> ➤ *Primary Variable:* **26) DIS AFRAM%**
> ➤ *View:* **Pie**

In 6 percent of the congressional districts, half the population or more is
African American. T F

In over 50 percent of the congressional districts, less than 6 percent of the
population is African American. T F

> *Data File:* **HOUSE106**
> *Task:* **Univariate**
> ➤ *Primary Variable:* **25) DIST HISP%**
> ➤ *View:* **Pie**

In about 4 percent of the congressional districts, half the population or more
is Hispanic. T F

6. Now let's see to what extent congresspersons are from the same racial/ethnic groups as their con-
    stituents.

> *Data File:* **HOUSE106**
> ➤ *Task:* **Cross-tabulation**
> ➤ *Row Variable:* **3) RACE/ETHNI**
> ➤ *Column Variable:* **26) DIS AFRAM%**
> ➤ *View:* **Table**
> ➤ *Display:* **Column %**

Copy the *second row* of the percentaged table. (Just ignore the message about a potential significance problem; this is not actually a problem here since we are using all 435 representatives rather
than a sample of representatives.)

	0–5%	6%–14%	15%–49%	50% OR +
AFRICAN-AM	_____%	_____%	_____%	_____%

Data File: **HOUSE106**
Task: **Cross-tabulation**
Row Variable: **3) RACE/ETHNI**
➤ Column Variable: **25) DIST HISP%**
➤ View: **Table**
➤ Display: **Column %**

Copy the *third row* of the percentaged table.

	UNDER 3%	3%–9%	10%–49%	50% OR +
HISPANIC	_____%	_____%	_____%	_____%

Circle the letter of the statement that best summarizes the results of these two tables.

   a.   Congresspersons are very likely to share the race or ethnicity of their constituents.

   b.   The racial and ethnic composition of a district appears to have little effect on the race or ethnicity of the person elected to Congress.

   c.   Race/ethnicity appears to have an effect in Hispanic districts, but not in African American districts, suggesting that language differences may be more important than racial differences.

7. In addition to affinity groups, there are organized groups who work to influence public opinion and public officials. Many groups track bills in Congress that affect their constituencies and rate members of Congress based on their support of or opposition to particular bills. Let's look at one of these ratings. The American Civil Liberties Union (ACLU) rated members of Congress on their votes on several different bills. Two of these bills were 44) FLAG DESCR and 45) STATEABORT. On each bill, the ACLU supported a negative vote.

Let's look at the effect of the person's party on this rating.

Data File: **HOUSE106**
Task: **Cross-tabulation**
➤ Row Variable: **27) ACLU RATE**
➤ Column Variable: **9) PARTY**
➤ View: **Table**
➤ Display: **Column %**

Copy the *second* row of the percentaged table.

	DEMOCRAT	REPUBLICAN
HIGH	_____%	_____%

What is the value of V for this table?   V = _____

Is V statistically significant?   Yes   No

Republican and Democratic members of Congress are equally likely to get high ratings from the ACLU.   T   F

8. While the ACLU focuses on one area (civil liberties issues), some organized interest groups concern themselves with a broad spectrum of political issues. For example, on the conservative end of the spectrum, the American Conservative Union (ACU) rates members of Congress in terms of a wide variety of issues. Let's see how the political party affiliations of representatives relate to the ACU ratings.

> Data File: **HOUSE106**
> Task: **Cross-tabulation**
> ➤ Row Variable: **29) ACU RATE**
> ➤ Column Variable: **9) PARTY**
> ➤ View: **Table**
> ➤ Display: **Column %**

Make sure to read the variable description for ACU RATE and then answer the following questions.

What is the value of Cramer's V for this table?   V = _____

Is V statistically significant?   Yes   No

Republican members of Congress are overwhelmingly conservative by the ACU ratings, and Democratic members are overwhelmingly liberal.   T   F

The ACU ratings of representatives tend to be high (conservative) or low (liberal) rather than in between.   T   F

9. Let's see whether liberals or conservatives have the advantage in attracting PAC money.

> Data File: **HOUSE106**
> Task: **Cross-tabulation**
> ➤ Row Variable: **20) %PAC CONTR**
> ➤ Column Variable: **29) ACU RATE**
> ➤ View: **Table**
> ➤ Display: **Column %**

What is the value of Cramer's V for this table?   V = _____

Is V statistically significant?   Yes   No

Which group received the highest percentage of its campaign funds from PACs? (Circle one.)   Liberals

                                                                                Moderates

                                                                                Conservatives

Part IV

INSTITUTIONS

Everyone talks about "the government." It's too big, too expensive, too conservative, too intrusive, too unresponsive—but, what *is* the government? Is it politicians, bureaucrats, judges, elected officials, or what? In the United States, it is all of these things.

The American government consists of three branches, or institutions: the legislative, the executive, and the judicial. The first consists of the Senate and the House of Representatives. The primary purpose of the legislative branch is to *enact* laws. The executive branch is headed by the president and includes all of the millions of employees who staff the government agencies. The primary purpose of the executive branch is to *administer* the laws. The judicial branch of government consists of federal courts, headed by the Supreme Court. Its primary purpose is to *interpret and apply* the laws.

In the next four exercises you will explore the institutions of our government.

THE CONGRESS

All legislative powers herein granted shall be vested in a Congress of the United States.

ARTICLE I, UNITED STATES
CONSTITUTION

Tasks: Mapping, Univariate, Cross-Tabulation, Historical Trends
Data Files: STATES, HOUSE106, HISTORY, GSS

This table shows the number of members of the U.S. House of Representatives from each state in 2000. California has the most, 52. New York is second highest with 31, just barely ahead of Texas with 30, followed by Florida (23), Pennsylvania (21), and Illinois (20).

➤ *Data File:* **STATES**
➤ *Task:* **Mapping**
➤ *Variable 1:* **91) # HOUSE**
➤ *View:* **List: Rank**

RANK	CASE NAME	VALUE
1	California	52
2	New York	31
3	Texas	30
4	Florida	23
5	Pennsylvania	21
6	Illinois	20
7	Ohio	19
8	Michigan	16
9	New Jersey	13
10	North Carolina	12

Membership in the House is based on population, so the more populous states have the most members. Because the number of seats in the House has been fixed at 435, and because states often grow or decline and their populations change relative to one another, seats are reapportioned every ten years. Reapportionment takes place the year after the census and goes into effect in the next election. The reapportionment from the 2000 census will start with the 2002 elections. However, no state, no matter how small its population, may be denied at least 1 representative.

➤ *Data File:* **HISTORY**
  ➤ *Task:* **Historical Trends**
➤ *Variable:* **15) APPORTION**

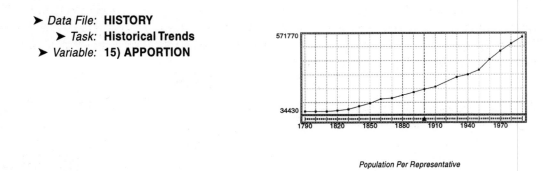

Population Per Representative

In 1790, each U.S. representative represented about 34,000 people. As the nation's population grew, the number of representatives increased until it was decided that no more representatives would be added. Thus, each representative today represents about 600,000 people.

In the following discussion, we'll look at certain features of the House of Representatives and use the members of the 106th Congress (elected in November 1998) to demonstrate these features.

➤ *Data File:* **HOUSE106**
  ➤ *Task:* **Univariate**
➤ *Primary Variable:* **9) PARTY**
  ➤ *View:* **Pie**

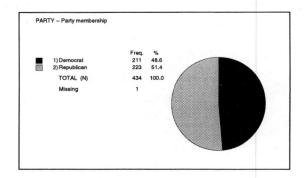

The first feature to note is that the House is currently split fairly evenly between Republicans and Democrats. Up until the 1994 election, Democrats had outnumbered Republicans in the House for 40 years—by substantial margins for most of that time. Then the 1994 election dramatically shifted power to the Republican Party. In the 104th Congress (1995–1996), Republicans outnumbered Democrats 235 to 199. In the 105th Congress (1997–1998), Republicans continued to outnumber Democrats 230 to 204. In the 106th Congress (1998–2000), Republicans continued to outnumber Democrats but only by a margin of 223 to 211. The 2000 elections resulted in a similar 222 to 211 margin.

Note that the numbers of Democrats and Republicans do not add up to 435. The 106th Congress began with one Independent (Bernard Sanders of Vermont). Thus, when we examine House votes on bills by party, the results will be off by one because Representative Sanders is excluded from that type of analysis. Also, on almost any bill there will be some representatives who do not vote. Thus, the number of ayes and nays might not add up to 435 on a particular bill. In the analysis of the HOUSE106 data file, there are several other reasons why the results concerning vote totals on a bill might not add up to 435 or might not break down by party completely in accord with the official results. First, Representative George Brown died and was replaced; however, since Representative Brown began the term and voted on many of the bills in the HOUSE106 data file, he (rather than his replacement) has been kept in the date file. Second, Representative Michael Forbes began the 106th Congress as a Republican but switched to the Democratic Party, but he is still coded as a Republican in this data file because he was still a Republican for many of the votes included in the HOUSE106 data file. Third, Representative Virgil Goode started the 106th Congress as a Democrat but switched later to Independent, but he is still coded as a Democrat here because he was a Democrat for many of the votes included in the HOUSE106 data file.

Data File: **HOUSE106**
Task: **Univariate**
➤ Primary Variable: **11) INCUMBENT**
➤ View: **Pie**

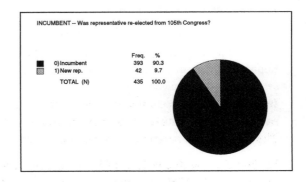

A second feature of Congress is the power of incumbency. We see here that 90.3 percent of the representatives in the 106th Congress were incumbents who were reelected. Thus, once a representative wins election to the House, the probability is extremely high that he or she can get reelected. This probability is even higher than it first appears, because some of the representatives in the previous Congress simply retired and did not run for reelection. In the elections of 2000, more than 400 House members chose to run for reelection and over 98 percent of them won.

Let's use the Second Congressional District in Indiana as a case study. In the November 2000 election, Mike Pence (a conservative Republican) won this congressional seat in a three-way contest against a conservative Democrat and another conservative Republican who ran as an Independent after failing to win the Republican nomination. Now that Pence has won his first election, how long will he be able to stay in Congress? He will probably stay in Congress until

- he decides to run for a different office—as did his predecessor (David McIntosh) who gave up the seat to make an unsuccessful run for the governor's office; or

- he decides to retire—as did his predecessor's predecessor (Phil Sharp); or

- he gets swept away by political events—as his predecessor's predecessor's predecessor (David Dennis) did.

Let's trace this sequence back to 1974 when David Dennis, a conservative Republican, was the representative in this area. Representative Dennis had served a number of terms and seemed destined to serve for a long time to come. However, he was swept away by national events—the Watergate scandal and his continuing defense of President Nixon long after many other Republicans in Congress decided that Nixon should resign or be impeached. Representative Dennis's opponent in 1974 was Phil Sharp, a moderate Democrat who had twice before run against Dennis. This time, Phil Sharp won—as did a number of other Democratic congressional candidates across the country whose Republican opponents were hurt by the Watergate scandal.

Despite winning initially because of Watergate, Representative Sharp won reelection nine more times before deciding to retire. How did a moderate Democrat win reelection in a fairly conservative, Republican district? First, he took moderate stands on many of the issues and conservative stands on some. Second, he provided a great number of constituency services. Third, given the short two-year term of representatives, Representative Sharp—like many representatives are forced to do—carried on a virtually constant campaign and outdid his opponents. Fourth, in campaign messages and in debates with his opponents, Sharp had the insider's advantage—knowledge of the workings of Congress, bills that had been considered, etc.

When Sharp retired, the district again elected a conservative Republican, David McIntosh. In 1994, as indicated previously, events were sweeping away a number of incumbent Democrats (but no incumbent Republican lost in 1994). The country elected a number of additional Republicans to Congress and switched power from the Democrats to the Republicans. Representative McIntosh was easily reelected several times, but he decided in 2000 to run for governor. That's when Mike Pence (who had twice run against Representative Sharp) ran and won.

Data File:	**HOUSE106**	
➤ *Task:*	**Cross-tabulation**	
➤ *Row Variable:*	**39) CENSUS REV**	
➤ *Column Variable:*	**9) PARTY**	
➤ *View:*	**Table**	
➤ *Display:*	**Column %**	

CENSUS REV   by   PARTY
Cramer's V: 0.977 **

		PARTY			
		Democrat	Republican	Missing	TOTAL
CENSUS REV	No	204	1	1	205
		98.1%	0.5%		47.9%
	Yes	4	219	0	223
		1.9%	99.5%		52.1%
	Missing	3	3	0	6
	TOTAL	208	220	1	428
		100.0%	100.0%		

Another feature of Congress is that party affiliation is a very important determinant of how representatives vote on many bills. While there are many routine, noncontroversial bills in Congress on which Republicans and Democrats are not different from one another, there is a substantial percentage of bills that find a majority of Republicans on one side and a majority of Democrats on the other side. Here we see that almost all Democrats voted against this census review bill and almost all Republicans voted for it. The differences between Democrats and Republicans are not this sharp on most bills, but there are definite patterns. In a previous exercise, we examined American Civil Liberties Union ratings of members of Congress and we examined some American Conservative Union (ACU) ratings. Let's now examine the liberal Americans for Democratic Action (ADA) ratings of members of Congress by party.

Data File:	**HOUSE106**	
Task:	**Cross-tabulation**	
➤ *Row Variable:*	**28) ADA RATE**	
➤ *Column Variable:*	**9) PARTY**	
➤ *View:*	**Table**	
➤ *Display:*	**Column %**	

ADA RATE   by   PARTY
Cramer's V: 0.883 **

		PARTY			
		Democrat	Republican	Missing	TOTAL
ADA RATE	Conservtve	1	174	0	175
		0.5%	78.0%		40.4%
	Middle	40	48	0	88
		19.0%	21.5%		20.3%
	Liberal	169	1	1	170
		80.5%	0.4%		39.3%
	Missing	1	0	0	1
	TOTAL	210	223	1	433
		100.0%	100.0%		

If you read the variable description, you see that we have categorized members of Congress in terms of ADA scores as follows. Representatives whose scores are 0 to 24 percent are classified as conservatives.

Those whose scores are 25 percent to 75 percent are classified as middle of the road. Those whose scores are 76 percent to 100 percent are classified as liberals. Given this classification, we see that all but about one fifth of the Democrats are liberals and all but about one-fifth of the Republicans are conservatives. Approximately one-fifth of the members of each party are in the middle of the road category. If we were to use the American Conservative Union ratings, the results would be very similar.

Data File: **HOUSE106**
Task: **Cross-tabulation**
➤ Row Variable: **41) REL ESTAB**
➤ Column Variable: **29) ACU RATE**
➤ View: **Table**
➤ Display: **Column %**

REL ESTAB   by   ACU RATE
Cramer's V: 0.878 **

| | | ACU RATE | | | | |
		Liberal	Middle	Conservtve	Missing	TOTAL
REL ESTAB	No	168	20	1	0	189
		95.5%	22.7%	0.6%		44.3%
	Yes	8	68	162	0	238
		4.5%	77.3%	99.4%		55.7%
	Missing	4	2	1	1	8
	TOTAL	176	88	163	1	427
		100.0%	100.0%	100.0%		

Interest groups such as the ADA or the ACU base their ratings of members of Congress on how representatives vote on bills. These ratings are also highly predictive of how representatives will vote on other bills that concern the general liberal-conservative dimension. Here, for example, we see that (using categories based on the American Conservative Union ratings) almost all liberals voted against this bill concerning a religious establishment issue and almost all conservatives voted for it.

Data File: **HOUSE106**
➤ Task: **Univariate**
➤ Primary Variable: **28) ADA RATE**
➤ View: **Bar Freq.**

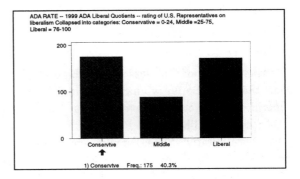

The next feature of Congress that we want to explore is whether members of Congress are more ideologically split than the general public is. We need to emphasize that we cannot directly and completely answer this question with the results used here, but we can explore it. Look at the distribution of ADA scores for all members of the House of Representatives. Even though the middle-of-the-road category includes scores from 25 percent to 75 percent, only one-fifth of the representatives are in the ideologically middle category. For exploratory comparison, we can look at the ideological self-classifications of the general public.

> ➤ *Data File:* **GSS**
> ➤ *Task:* **Univariate**
> ➤ *Primary Variable:* **5) LIB./CONS,**
> ➤ *View:* **Bar Freq.**

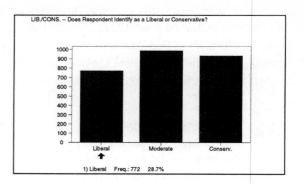

In the general public, we see that the biggest group is the middle group, those who classified themselves as moderates. While there are serious limitations in comparing the House results with these general public results, a look at the two distributions does support the idea that ideological differences among U.S. representatives are sharper than ideological differences within the general public.

> ➤ *Data File:* **HOUSE106**
> ➤ *Task:* **Cross-tabulation**
> ➤ *Row Variable:* **29) ACU RATE**
> ➤ *Column Variable:* **2) SEX**
> ➤ *View:* **Table**
> ➤ *Display:* **Column %**

ACU RATE by SEX
Cramer's V: 0.232 **

		SEX		
		Male	Female	TOTAL
ACU RATE	Liberal	141	39	180
		37.3%	69.6%	41.5%
	Middle	80	10	90
		21.2%	17.9%	20.7%
	Conservtve	157	7	164
		41.5%	12.5%	37.8%
	Missing	1	0	1
	TOTAL	378	56	434
		100.0%	100.0%	

Another feature of Congress is that the background characteristics of representatives can also affect how they vote. So far we have good indications that members of Congress are usually either fairly liberal or fairly conservative and that these ideological differences are related to party affiliation (Democrats are liberal and Republicans are conservative). Here we see that gender is also related to how representatives vote: Female representatives are more liberal than male representatives are. Is this because women are more likely to be Democrats? Let's check.

> *Data File:* **HOUSE106**
> *Task:* **Cross-tabulation**
> ➤ *Row Variable:* **9) PARTY**
> ➤ *Column Variable:* **2) SEX**
> ➤ *View:* **Table**
> ➤ *Display:* **Column %**

PARTY by SEX
Cramer's V: 0.162 **

		SEX		
		Male	Female	TOTAL
PARTY	Democrat	172	39	211
		45.5%	69.6%	48.6%
	Republican	206	17	223
		54.5%	30.4%	51.4%
	Missing	1	0	1
	TOTAL	378	56	434
		100.0%	100.0%	

We see here that a majority of women in Congress are Democrats and a majority of men are Republicans. So, the party difference might account for why women are more liberal than men in Congress. Let's see whether women are more liberal than men *within* the parties.

Data File: **HOUSE106**
Task: **Cross-tabulation**
➤ Row Variable: **29) ACU RATE**
➤ Column Variable: **2) SEX**
➤ Control Variable: **9) PARTY (Democrat)**
➤ View: **Table**
➤ Display: **Column %**

ACU RATE   by   SEX
Controls: PARTY: Democrat
Cramer's V: 0.169
Warning: Potential significance problem. Check row and column totals.

		SEX		
		Male	Female	TOTAL
ACU RATE	Liberal	140	38	178
		81.9%	97.4%	84.8%
	Middle	29	1	30
		17.0%	2.6%	14.3%
	Conservtve	2	0	2
		1.2%	0.0%	1.0%
	Missing	1	0	1
	TOTAL	171	39	210
		100.0%	100.0%	

The option for selecting a control variable is located on the same screen you use to select other variables. For this example, select 9) PARTY as a control variable and then click [OK] to continue as usual. Separate tables showing the relationship between the ACU ratings and gender will be shown for Democrats and Republicans.

By specifying PARTY as a control variable, we will obtain two tables: one table for Democrats and one for Republicans. The first table is for Democrats. Among Democrats, we see that 97.4 percent of women are liberals, which is higher than the 81.9 percent of men who are liberals. Now let's look at the Republican table. We do this by clicking the right arrow under the phrase "Control 1 of 2" on the left side of the screen.

Data File: **HOUSE106**
Task: **Cross-tabulation**
Row Variable: **29) ACU RATE**
Column Variable: **2) SEX**
➤ Control Variable: **9) PARTY (Republican)**
➤ View: **Table**
➤ Display: **Column %**

ACU RATE   by   SEX
Controls: PARTY: Republican
Cramer's V: 0.294 **
Warning: Potential significance problem. Check row and column totals.

		SEX		
		Male	Female	TOTAL
ACU RATE	Liberal	0	1	1
		0.0%	5.9%	0.4%
	Middle	51	9	60
		24.8%	52.9%	26.9%
	Conservtve	155	7	162
		75.2%	41.2%	72.6%
	TOTAL	206	17	223
		100.0%	100.0%	

Among Republicans, we see that while there is only one liberal (a woman), a higher percentage of women than men are in the middle category. As a result, 75.2 percent of the male Republicans are conservatives, but only 41.2 percent of women are in the conservative category.

Thus, among both Democrats and Republicans, women in Congress are more liberal (or less conservative) than men are. Now let's examine the effects of region on voting behavior.

Data File: **HOUSE106**
Task: **Cross-tabulation**
➤ Row Variable: **38) MISL DEFEN**
➤ Column Variable: **15) REGION**
➤ View: **Table**
➤ Display: **Column %**

MISL DEFEN   by   REGION
Cramer's V: 0.287 **

		REGION				
		Northeast	Midwest	South	West	TOTAL
MISL DEFEN	No	34	33	12	26	105
		39.1%	33.0%	8.3%	28.6%	24.9%
	Yes	53	67	132	65	317
		60.9%	67.0%	91.7%	71.4%	75.1%
	Missing	1	5	5	2	13
	TOTAL	87	100	144	91	422
		100.0%	100.0%	100.0%	100.0%	

Note: Before selecting the variables for this analysis, it would be a good idea to click the [Clear All] option to clear all the previous analysis, including the control variable.

Here we see that region can affect how representatives vote on particular issues. In this situation, Southern representatives were much more likely to vote for this missile defense system bill than were representatives of other regions, and Northeastern representatives were less likely to vote for the bill. Sometimes there has been a coalition (the "conservative coalition") of Republicans and some Southern Democrats against non-Southern Democrats. Does this coalition still exist now that Republicans control Congress? Let's examine votes on this bill broken down by three categories: Democrats, Southern Democrats, and Republicans.

Data File: **HOUSE106**
Task: **Cross-tabulation**
Row Variable: **38) MISL DEFEN**
➤ Column Variable: **10) SOUTH DEM**
➤ View: **Table**
➤ Display: **Column %**

MISL DEFEN   by   SOUTH DEM
Cramer's V: 0.616 **

		SOUTH DEM				
		Democrat	S.Democrat	Republican	Missing	TOTAL
MISL DEFEN	No	86	11	7	1	104
		61.9%	18.3%	3.2%		24.7%
	Yes	53	49	215	0	317
		38.1%	81.7%	96.8%		75.3%
	Missing	4	2	7	0	13
	TOTAL	139	60	222	1	421
		100.0%	100.0%	100.0%		

A strong majority of Southern Democrats (81.7 percent) and a strong majority of Republicans (96.8 percent) supported this bill while a majority of non-Southern Democrats (61.9 percent) opposed the bill. Thus, the "conservative coalition" is still very much alive in Congress.

Politics concerns making decisions about matters over which there is conflict and disagreement. Thus, many bills in Congress are passed with a majority of Democrats on one side and a majority of Republicans on the other side. However, a final feature of Congress that we want to stress is that the members of Congress sometimes reach a consensus or nearly a consensus. There are several bills included in the HOUSE106 file in which substantial majorities of both parties voted together. Let's finish by looking at the distribution of votes on a bill to amend the Social Security Act to eliminate the earnings test for individuals who have attained retirement age.

Data File: **HOUSE106**
➤ Task: **Univariate**
➤ Primary Variable: **67) SENIORWORK**
➤ View: **Pie**

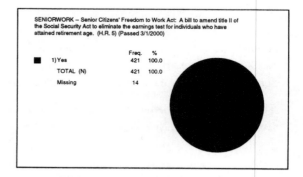

How's that for a concensus? Every representative who voted on this bill voted for it.

Your turn.

EXERCISE **13**

THE PRESIDENCY

[S]hould my administration prove to be a very wicked one, or what is more probable, a very foolish one, if you, the people, are true to yourselves and the Constitution, there is little harm I can do, thank God.
ABRAHAM LINCOLN, 1861

Tasks: Mapping, Univariate, Cross-Tabulation
Data Files: STATES, USPRES

The American presidency was invented by the Constitutional Convention. Never before had a nation been led by a freely elected chief executive with powers independent of the legislative branch of government. In all other democracies at that time, and nearly all of them since, executive power was vested in the leader of the legislature; if we were to adopt that system, the Speaker of the House of Representatives would be the chief executive. Only a handful of nations, all of them in North and South America, follow the American model of an elected, independent executive who is in charge of the entire executive branch of government.

Because the American presidency has so much authority and so many independent resources, the delegates at the Constitutional Convention were very worried about the wrong sort of person gaining office. That's why they created the electoral college. They never meant for presidents to be elected by popular vote. Instead, they wanted presidents to be selected by a few of the nation's most informed and concerned leaders. Thus, Alexander Hamilton explained in 1788 that the process of selection by the electoral college "affords a moral certainty that the office will never fall to the lot of any man who is not in an eminent degree endowed with the requisite qualification."

While vestiges of the electoral college remain, these days popular vote pretty much decides who becomes president, with the 2000 election being a major exception. Over the previous 100 years, the electoral college vote mirrored the popular vote, but even when this occurred, the electoral college still had subtle effects on who became president. So, let's see how well the system has worked.

> *Data File:* **STATES**
>   ➤ *Task:* **Mapping**
> ➤ *Variable 1:* **88) PRESIDENTS**
>   ➤ *View:* **List: Rank**

RANK	CASE NAME	VALUE
1	New York	7
1	Ohio	7
3	Virginia	5
4	Massachusetts	4
5	Texas	3
5	California	3
5	Tennessee	3
8	Pennsylvania	1
8	Louisiana	1
8	Kansas	1

Here we see the home states of each of the 43 presidents, from George Washington to George W. Bush (although Bush was the 42nd person to hold the office, the record books refer to him as the 43rd president because they count Grover Cleveland twice since his two terms of office were not consecutive).

The eastern bias is clear. More than half of all presidents have come from four states: Ohio (7), New York (7), Virginia (5), and Massachusetts (4). Eleven states have had only one president, and 32 have had none. Two major factors have played a role: population size and when states entered the union. In the beginning, only a few states *could* produce presidents because there were only 14 states. Thus, New York, Virginia, and Massachusetts were electing presidents long before most other states existed. Moreover, even in the days when the electoral college actually met and chose a president, population size mattered a lot since each state's votes were proportionate to its population. In 1790 Virginia was by far the most populous state being twice as large as second-place Pennsylvania, hence its many presidents—including George Washington and Thomas Jefferson. New York's many presidents can be traced to the fact that it too was one of the original states and soon became by far the most populous state (it was not until the early 1960s that California had more people than New York, and Texas did not pass New York until the 1990s).

That leaves Ohio. How did it elect seven presidents? There are three factors: age, population, and location. Ohio is an old state, having entered the union in 1803, and it soon became one of the most populous states, ranking fourth largest in the latter 19th century. But of even greater importance is location. Ohio is the most eastern state of the Midwest, so its politicians often mediated conflicts between the East and the more westerly areas, which was an advantage for its presidential candidates. They were acceptable to all regions—so much so that in the 1920 election the winner was the Republican senator from Ohio (Harding) and the loser was the governor of Ohio (Cox).

> *Data File:* **STATES**
>   *Task:* **Mapping**
> *Variable 1:* **88) PRESIDENTS**
> ➤ *Variable 2:* **2) POPULATION**
>   ➤ *Views:* **Map**

PRESIDENTS -- Number of United States Presidents

r = 0.588**

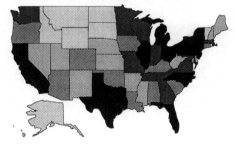

POPULATION -- Population in Thousands (1990 Census)

Even though populations have changed a lot through the decades, there still is a strong and significant correlation between the number of presidents a state has produced and its population.

Now, let's see what sorts of people have been president. For one thing, they all have been males. A woman ran for vice president in 1984, but as yet no woman has been nominated for president by a major party. But what about other features of the American presidency?

➤ *Data File:* **USPRES**
➤ *Task:* **Univariate**
➤ *Primary Variable:* **6) PARTY**
➤ *View:* **Pie**

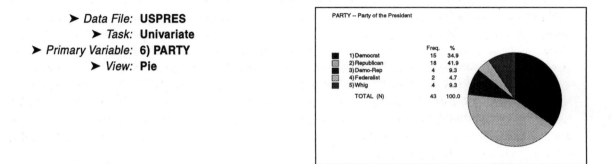

PARTY -- Party of the President

	Freq.	%
1) Democrat	15	34.9
2) Republican	18	41.9
3) Demo-Rep	4	9.3
4) Federalist	2	4.7
5) Whig	4	9.3
TOTAL (N)	43	100.0

This data file consists of the 43 presidents. Here we see their party affiliations. There have been 15 Democrats and 18 Republicans. But that leaves 10 others. The Federalists were an antiparty party. The name was applied to the opponents of political parties as divisive "factions," including George Washington, who devoted much of his farewell address to condemning parties: "Let me warn you in the most solemn manner against the baneful effects of the spirit of party."

The Federalist name was adopted by Alexander Hamilton to clarify opposition to the party formed by Thomas Jefferson, who was as ardently in favor of parties as Washington was against them. Jefferson's party was called the Democratic-Republicans and they elected four early presidents, including Jefferson himself. When Andrew Jackson became a presidential candidate, the party shortened its name to the Democratic Party. Meanwhile, the name Federalist disappeared; the new opposition party came to be known as the Whigs, and they elected four presidents. During the 1850s the issue of slavery split both the Whigs and the Democrats, and the antislavery factions of each withdrew to form the Republican Party, whose first successful presidential candidate was Abraham Lincoln. Since 1853, all U.S. presidents have been either Democrats or Republicans.

Data File: **USPRES**
Task: **Univariate**
➤ Primary Variable: **17) YRS IN OFF**
➤ View: **Pie**

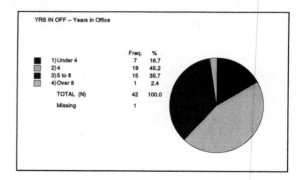

A presidential term in office is four years. Here we see that seven presidents served fewer than four years. These were either presidents who died in office or vice presidents who succeeded and then did not serve a term of their own. Nineteen presidents served but a single term, and 15 more began a second term (and most completed it). For 150 years no president ever sought a third term, modeling themselves on George Washington, who declined a third term. Indeed, as the Democratic Party platform put it in 1896, "We declare it to be the unwritten law of this Republic, established by custom and useage of one hundred years . . . that no man should be eligible for a third term of office."

After Franklin D. Roosevelt ran for and won third and fourth terms, the 22nd Amendment to the Constitution was adopted:

> No person shall be elected to the office of the President more than twice, and no person who has held the office of President, or acted as President, for more than two years of a term to which some other person was elected President shall be elected to the office of President more than once.

Presidents have many formal and informal powers. One of their formal powers is the ability to veto legislation passed by Congress. President Washington vetoed only two pieces of legislation during his two terms in office. President Franklin Delano Roosevelt cast the most vetoes—at 635. He, however, was president for 14 years. Dividing 635 by 14 reveals that Roosevelt cast an average of 45 vetoes for each year in office.

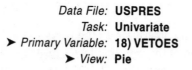

Data File: **USPRES**
Task: **Univariate**
➤ Primary Variable: **18) VETOES**
➤ View: **Pie**

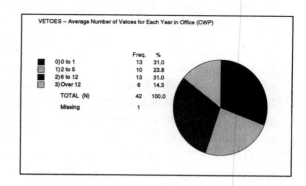

Here we see that about one-third of the presidents cast no more than one veto for each year in office, one-quarter of the presidents cast between two and five vetoes each year, another third vetoed six to twelve pieces of legislation each year, and 14 percent vetoed twelve or more bills for every year in office.

Data File: **USPRES**
➤ Task: **Cross-tabulation**
➤ Row Variable: **18) VETOES**
➤ Column Variable: **35) ERA**
➤ View: **Table**
➤ Display: **Column %**

VETOES   by   ERA
Cramer's V: 0.815 **
Warning: Potential significance problem. Check row and column totals.

	ERA		
	Pre CW	Post CW	TOTAL
0 to 1	12	1	13
	75.0%	3.8%	31.0%
2 to 5	4	6	10
	25.0%	23.1%	23.8%
6 to 12	0	13	13
	0.0%	50.0%	31.0%
Over 12	0	6	6
	0.0%	23.1%	14.3%
Missing	0	1	1
TOTAL	16	26	42
	100.0%	100.0%	

Presidents up until the time of the Civil War were quite reluctant to use the veto power. As mentioned previously, George Washington cast only two vetoes. John Adams, Thomas Jefferson, John Quincy Adams, William Harrison, Zachary Taylor, and Millard Fillmore did not veto any legislation. Three-quarters of the pre–Civil War presidents cast either no vetoes or less than one veto for each year in office. None of these presidents averaged more than five vetoes per year. Since the Civil War, half of the presidents have cast between six and twelve vetoes for each year in office.

Presidential vetoes may be considered a sign of a strong presidency or a weak presidency. Franklin Delano Roosevelt was one of the strongest presidents in U.S. history, convincing Congress to pass his New Deal programs. Yet, Roosevelt often resorted to using vetoes as well. Thus, some great presidents use the veto power to further increase their influence. On the other hand, vetoes also may be a sign of presidential weakness. A stronger president should be able to influence Congress during the early stages of the legislative process, such that bills the president finds objectionable do not pass Congress. Gerald Ford succeeded to the presidency after the resignation of President Richard Nixon. Ford was never elected president and thus could not claim a popular mandate. He also faced a Congress controlled by the opposition party. Ford had little influence over Congress and used the presidential veto 66 times. Many of Ford's vetoes, additionally, were overturned by Congress.

Congress can vacate a presidential veto with two-thirds votes in both the U.S. House of Representatives and the Senate. With a super-majority vote required in both houses of Congress, over-rides of presidential vetoes are rare. Less than 5 percent of vetoes are overturned by Congress. Perhaps a surer sign of presidential weakness is the percent of vetoes overridden.

Data File: **USPRES**
➤ Task: **Univariate**
➤ Primary Variable: **29) OVERRIDE**
➤ View: **Pie**

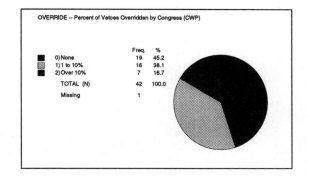

OVERRIDE -- Percent of Vetoes Overridden by Congress (CWP)

	Freq.	%
0) None	19	45.2
1) 1 to 10%	16	38.1
2) Over 10%	7	16.7
TOTAL (N)	42	100.0
Missing	1	

This chart shows that nearly half (45 percent) of presidents have had no vetoes overridden. But remember that a number of early presidents cast no vetoes and therefore could have no vetoes overridden. A more appropriate chart would examine only presidents from the post–Civil War era, when vetoes, and overrides of vetoes, are more common.

<table>
<tr><td align="right">Data File:</td><td>USPRES</td></tr>
<tr><td align="right">Task:</td><td>Univariate</td></tr>
<tr><td align="right">Primary Variable:</td><td>29) OVERRIDE</td></tr>
<tr><td align="right">➤ Subset Variable:</td><td>35) ERA</td></tr>
<tr><td align="right">➤ Subset Categories:</td><td>Include: 1) POST CW</td></tr>
<tr><td align="right">➤ View:</td><td>Pie</td></tr>
</table>

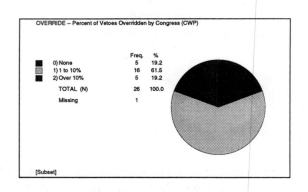

Looking only at presidents since the Civil War, we see that presidents can expect that between 1 and 10 percent of their vetoes will be overridden by Congress. Only five presidents have been able to sustain all of their vetoes, while five other presidents have seen more than 10 percent overturned.

Presidents attempt to influence the legislative process by proposing legislation, molding the national agenda, and signing or vetoing legislation. They influence the judicial branch through their appointment of judges. Presidents nominate potential judges, and the Senate typically confirms these nominees. Presidents nominate judges both to the Supreme Court and for all other federal courts. Once confirmed, these judges serve lifetime appointments. Thus, one of the legacies of any president is in the number of judges appointed. Let's first look at Supreme Court appointments.

<table>
<tr><td align="right">Data File:</td><td>USPRES</td></tr>
<tr><td align="right">Task:</td><td>Univariate</td></tr>
<tr><td align="right">➤ Primary Variable:</td><td>25) SUP CT</td></tr>
<tr><td align="right">➤ View:</td><td>Pie</td></tr>
</table>

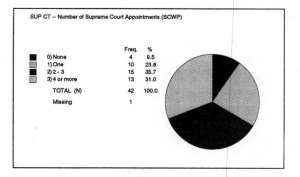

If you are replicating this pie chart, be sure to delete the subset variable from the previous example.

Four presidents were unable to appoint any Supreme Court judges, because no vacancies occurred on the Court during that president's term in office. President Jimmy Carter was one of these presidents who never had the opportunity to appoint a Supreme Court justice. Of the nine justices on the Supreme Court in January 2001, President Reagan appointed four, Presidents George Bush and Bill Clinton each appointed two, and one was appointed by President Ford. As the pie chart shows, most presidents can expect to appoint between one and three Supreme Court justices, but one-third of the presidents have been able to appoint four or more justices.

Data File: **USPRES**
Task: **Univariate**
➤ Primary Variable: **26) TOT JUDGES**
➤ View: **Pie**

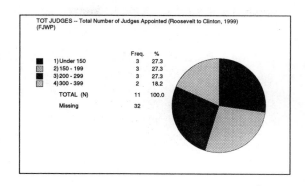

Presidents make many more judicial appointments to federal district courts or to the federal court of appeals. The pie chart above indicates the total number of judges appointed by presidents since Franklin Delano Roosevelt's presidency. As shown, presidents make hundreds of judicial appointments. Since presidents tend to appoint judges from their own political party, these presidential appointments shape the future decision making of the judicial branch.

Your turn.

THE BUREAUCRACY

The President ... may require the Opinion, in writing, of the principal Officer in each of the executive Departments, upon any Subject relating to the Duties of their respective Offices ... and by and with the Advice and Consent of the Senate, shall appoint Ambassadors, other public Ministers and Consuls, Judges of the supreme Court, and all other Officers of the United States, whose Appointments are not herein otherwise provided for, and which shall be established by Law: but the Congress may by Law vest the Appointment of such inferior Officers, as they think proper, in the President alone, in the Courts of Law, or in the Heads of Departments.

SECTION 2, ARTICLE II, UNITED STATES CONSTITUTION

Tasks: Mapping, Univariate, Cross-Tabulation, Historical Trends, Scatterplot
Data Files: STATES, GSS, NES, HISTORY, NATIONS

The section of the Constitution quoted above is *everything* the founders bothered to say about the executive branch of government, aside from the presidency. Nothing is said about a cabinet, about a State Department, or about any of the thousands of agencies that today constitute the federal government and often are referred to collectively as the bureaucracy. The reason the Constitution said so little about this aspect of government is that in those days the government was so little.

In traditional agrarian societies, such as those in Europe during medieval times, the government was nothing more than the king's or queen's household and court. Needed functionaries such as clerks, accountants, and tax collectors were servants of the crown, equal in status to the cooks, grooms, and butlers making up the royal household. When the ruler needed a general, an advisor, a chief justice, or an administrator of the treasury, one of the noble members of the court was asked to do the job. The nobles did not regard a government post as an occupation or even a full-time activity. Often they had no special qualifications beyond their noble birth and their social graces.

This system worked because governments in those days did very little. Beyond extracting taxes from the populace, maintaining a minimum of public order, and defending the realm against invaders, there was little to do. After all, more than 90 percent of the population led quiet rural lives without schools, post offices, roads, hospitals, or fire departments. Laws were simple. There were no regulatory agencies, no inspectors, and no *paperwork*—tax collectors used carts, not forms.

As the world became modern, this system could not suffice. With rapidly growing populations and the rise of industry, the demands on government grew. As a result, governments got much larger. And, as more and more people were needed to staff the government, the old selection methods became obsolete.

When George Washington took office as the first president of the United States, his first task was to appoint people to fill all of the jobs in the federal government including postmasters to manage all the local post offices. In making these appointments, Washington *personally* evaluated each person. How could he? Easily, there being fewer than 700 of them! For years, each time the political party in control of the American government changed, nearly all government employees were discharged and replaced with supporters of the new administration. Thus, when Thomas Jefferson took office, he fired hundreds of Federalists appointed by Presidents Washington and Adams and replaced them with his supporters. This practice was known as the **spoils system**: the spoils (or benefits) of public office go to the supporters of winning politicians. This system reached its height in American history when Andrew Jackson was elected and thousands of government employees were terminated.

Aside from corruption and other abuses, the spoils system was undesirable because it meant that many technical or otherwise complex jobs were continually being turned over to beginners. Eventually, the civil service system was introduced whereby people are hired and promoted on the basis of merit, not political connections, and they may be terminated only for sufficient cause.

Today, governments, like all *large organizations*, are **bureaucracies**. All bureaucracies have certain key features. They consist of a set of positions, each with very specific and often very specialized duties. These positions are administered on the basis of clearly specified lines of authority. Hiring and promotion are done on the basis of qualifications and training. Finally, and very important, careful, written records are kept of all communications and transactions.

Bureaucracies exist because they are the most efficient solution to the problems of coordinating and controlling the actions of large numbers of people involved in some common enterprise, whether it be managing General Motors or running the Department of Commerce.

The problem is that bureaucracies often develop goals of their own, and these may put them in conflict with the purposes for which the organization was created or with the interests of those whom it was intended to serve. This is why the words *bureaucrat* and *bureaucracy* carry unpleasant connotations, suggesting meddlesome people and muddled organizations. This is especially true when people speak of government bureaucracies. From all parties and nearly all candidates, complaints are directed toward government agencies and their millions of employees—the bureaucracy. It is too big, too wasteful, too arrogant, too powerful, and too inefficient.

Let's pursue some of these concerns.

➤ *Data File:* **STATES**
  ➤ *Task:* **Mapping**
➤ *Variable 1:* **18) FED.EMPLOY**
  ➤ *View:* **List: Rank**

RANK	CASE NAME	VALUE
1	Maryland	2740
2	Virginia	2562
3	Alaska	2550
4	Hawaii	2239
5	Utah	2034
6	New Mexico	1695
7	Colorado	1583
8	Oklahoma	1427
9	Montana	1406
10	Alabama	1385

Here we see that the federal bureaucracy is not confined to Washington DC. Among the states, Maryland and Virginia have the highest proportions of federal employees because so many agencies have moved to suburbs near Washington, thus becoming resident in these two states which surround the District. However, many other states far from Washington are high in federal employees. One reason is that they have many military installations. Members of the armed forces are not counted in these personnel figures, but military bases always employ a lot of civilians.

Obviously, the federal payroll has grown incredibly since the days of George Washington. Every state has many times more federal employees than made up the total number in 1789. Let's examine this growth.

➤ *Data File:* **HISTORY**
  ➤ *Task:* **Historical Trends**
➤ *Variables:* **53) NON-D EMP**

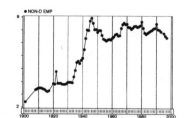

Non-defense executive branch employees per 1000 population

In 1900 there were slightly over 2 government employees per 1,000 population. Since the mid-sixties, this rate has been about 8 per 1,000. (Those employed in national defense are not included in these numbers.)

➤ *Data File:* **GSS**
  ➤ *Task:* **Univariate**
➤ *Primary Variable:* **31) FED.GOV'T**
  ➤ *View:* **Pie**

Here we see that although a third (36.4 percent) of Americans say they have only a low level of confidence in the federal government, a majority of Americans (63.6 percent) say they have at least some confidence—but only 14 percent (not shown) say they have a "great deal" of confidence. That is not a very powerful vote of confidence in our government. "Federal government" is, of course, a very inclusive concept. The focus of people's lack of confidence might be primarily the president, Congress, the courts, or the bureaucracy—or all four.

<table>
<tr><td>Data File:</td><td>GSS</td></tr>
<tr><td>➤ Task:</td><td>Cross-tabulation</td></tr>
<tr><td>➤ Row Variable:</td><td>31) FED.GOV'T</td></tr>
<tr><td>➤ Column Variable:</td><td>35) SUP.COURT?</td></tr>
<tr><td>➤ View:</td><td>Table</td></tr>
<tr><td>➤ Display:</td><td>Column %</td></tr>
</table>

FED.GOV'T   by   SUP.COURT?
Cramer's V: 0.285 **

		SUP.COURT?				
		Great deal	Only some	Hardly any	Missing	TOTAL
FED.GOV'T	Some conf	444	602	87	41	1133
		76.6%	63.8%	33.3%		63.5%
	Low conf	136	341	174	20	651
		23.4%	36.2%	66.7%		36.5%
	Missing	12	7	6	962	987
	TOTAL	580	943	261	1023	1784
		100.0%	100.0%	100.0%		

Clearly, people who lack confidence in the Supreme Court also tend to lack confidence in the federal government as a whole. Yet, 33.3 percent of those who said they have hardly any confidence in the Supreme Court did express some confidence in the government, and almost one of four who expressed a great deal of confidence in the Court expressed low confidence in the government.

<table>
<tr><td>Data File:</td><td>GSS</td></tr>
<tr><td>Task:</td><td>Cross-tabulation</td></tr>
<tr><td>Row Variable:</td><td>31) FED.GOV'T</td></tr>
<tr><td>➤ Column Variable:</td><td>36) CONGRESS?</td></tr>
<tr><td>➤ View:</td><td>Table</td></tr>
<tr><td>➤ Display:</td><td>Column %</td></tr>
</table>

FED.GOV'T   by   CONGRESS?
Cramer's V: 0.399 **

		CONGRESS?			
		Some conf	Low conf	Missing	TOTAL
FED.GOV'T	Some conf	956	195	23	1151
		76.4%	34.8%		63.6%
	Low conf	295	365	11	660
		23.6%	65.2%		36.4%
	Missing	20	11	956	987
	TOTAL	1251	560	990	1811
		100.0%	100.0%		

The same pattern holds for confidence in Congress. A lot of people have either some confidence in both the federal government and Congress or low confidence in both. Yet a substantial number of Americans express greater confidence in one than the other.

From this result we probably can conclude that, while many people interpreted the item about the federal government in a very general way, a significant number associated it more narrowly to refer to the bureaucracy. In any case, Americans have been losing confidence in their government according to any measure.

➤ *Data File:* **HISTORY**
   ➤ *Task:* **Historical Trends**
➤ *Variables:* **34) TRUST GOV**

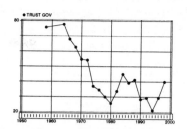

Percent who say they trust the government in Washington to do
what is right most of the time (survey data)

One might suppose that if people lack confidence in their government, they may become apathetic and cease to take part in politics. But it could be argued with equal plausibility that people who lack confidence will be more likely to vote because they want change.

➤ *Data File:* **GSS**
   ➤ *Task:* **Cross-tabulation**
  ➤ *Row Variable:* **20)VOTE 96?**
➤ *Column Variable:* **31) FED.GOV'T**
     ➤ *View:* **Table**
   ➤ *Display:* **Column %**

VOTE 96?   by   FED.GOV'T
Cramer's V: 0.001

		FED.GOV'T			
		Some conf	Low conf	Missing	TOTAL
VOTE 96?	Voted	725	430	628	1155
		68.1%	68.1%		68.1%
	Did not	340	201	289	541
		31.9%	31.9%		31.9%
	Missing	109	40	70	219
	TOTAL	1065	631	987	1696
		100.0%	100.0%		

Here we see that confidence in the federal government is unrelated to having voted in the 1996 presidential election—perhaps apathy and anger are cancelling one another out.

Your turn.

NAME:

COURSE:

DATE:

Workbook exercises and software are copyrighted. Copying is prohibited by law.

REVIEW QUESTIONS

Based on the first part of this exercise, answer True or False to the following items:

The civil service system also is called the spoils system.	T F
The secretary of agriculture is the only cabinet member mentioned in the Constitution.	T F
Thomas Jefferson participated in the spoils system.	T F
The principal defect of bureaucracies is that promotion usually is based on who you know.	T F
Large business organizations manage not to become bureaucracies.	T F

EXPLORIT QUESTIONS

1. According to the preliminary discussion, a sizable proportion of federal employees are used to staff military installations. Let's look at the relationship between the per capita Defense Department expenditures and the federal employment rate across states.

> *Data File:* **STATES**
> *Task:* **Scatterplot**
> *Dependent Variable:* **18) FED.EMPLOY**
> *Independent Variable:* **19) DEFENSE $**
> *View:* **Reg. Line**

r = _____   Significant? Yes No

This result fails to support the idea that the greater the military presence in a state, the higher the federal employment rate.   T   F

2. Many people are concerned about the growth of government. Let's look at government growth in more detail.

> *Data File:* **HISTORY**
> *Task:* **Historical Trends**
> *Variables:* **49) FED EMP RT**

Government employment seems to

    a.   have increased at a relatively constant rate.

    b.   have spikes at certain short periods.

    c.   have had little change over time.

Scrolling through the events listed at the bottom, which of the following events seem to have had the greatest impact on the government employment rate?

    a.   presidential elections

    b.   wars

    c.   new inventions

    d.   constitutional amendments

3.   Let's separate defense employment from nondefense government employment.

       Data File: **HISTORY**
           Task: **Historical Trends**
    ➤ *Variables:* **50) DEF EMP RT**
                  53) NON-D EMP

Wars affect defense employment but have relatively little impact on other types of government employment.   T   F

Since the Vietnam War ended in 1974, the defense employment rate has slowly declined.   T   F

The nondefense government employment rate has remained fairly constant since the mid-sixties.   T   F

Except for wartime, nondefense employment is higher than defense employment.   T   F

4.   Government outlays over time also reflect the relative growth of various segments of government.

       Data File: **HISTORY**
           Task: **Historical Trends**
    ➤ *Variables:* **54) DEF$/POP**
                  55) HR$/POP

What is the description of 54) DEF$/POP?

_____

_____

What is the description of 55) HR$/POP?

_____

_____

Spending on human resources has been growing since the late sixties.　　　　T　　F

Since the mid-eighties, spending on national defense has been fairly stable.　　　　T　　F

5.　Let's look at a finer breakdown on the human resources expenditures. These are some of the categories that are included in human resources:

> Data File:　**HISTORY**
> Task:　**Historical Trends**
> ➤ Variables:　**56) S.S.$/POP**
> 　　　　　**57) I.S.$/POP**
> 　　　　　**58) MED$/POP**

What is the description of 56) S.S.$/POP?

_____

_____

What is the description of 57) I.S.$/POP?

_____

_____

What is the description of 58) MED$/POP?

_____

_____

Describe how the outlays in these categories have changed since 1940. What do you expect to happen to these outlays in the next 20 years?

6. The federal government is not the only level of government that has bureaucracies. State and local
    governments also have bureaucracies and provide many complementary services to the federal gov-
    ernment. Both levels of government have agencies responsible for schools, transportation, crime pre-
    vention, and a host of other government functions. Let's examine health care spending by the 50
    state governments. The specific variable in the STATES file looks at health care spending per capita,
    i.e., the dollar amount spent per state resident.

    > *Data File:* **STATES**
    > *Task:* **Mapping**
    > *Variable 1:* **109) HLTH$/CAP**
    > *View:* **List: Rank**

	STATE	DOLLARS
State that spends the highest dollar amount per state resident.	_____	_____
State that spends the lowest dollar amount per state resident.	_____	_____

    One reason states may vary in health expenditures is the types of preferences found in the popula-
    tion. In general, Democrats tend to prefer more government spending on social welfare programs,
    whereas Republicans tend to prefer less government spending on such programs. Let's add a mea-
    sure of the partisanship of each state's residents to see if this can explain variations in state expendi-
    tures on health programs.

          Data File: **STATES**
          Task: **Mapping**
          Variable 1: **109) HLTH$/CAP**
    > *Variable 2:* **171) POP-DEM**
    > *View:* **Map**

    What is the correlation between Democratic citizenry and state spending on
    health programs? $r =$ _____

    Is it statistically significant?   Yes   No

7. Nations also vary in their level of government support for health care. Many of the industrialized
    nations provide their citizens with health insurance. In the United States health insurance is privately
    funded. Let's see how the U.S. compares to other industrial countries in total spending (both private
    and government spending) per capita on health care.

➤ *Data File:* **NATIONS**
➤ *Task:* **Mapping**
➤ *Variable 1:* **41) HEALTH**
➤ *View:* **List: Rank**

RANK

U.S. ranking on total (private and public) spending on health care as a
percentage of GDP (gross domestic product)   _____

Now let's look at how the United States ranks on government spending on health care. The variable
in the NATIONS data set calculates the percentage of total health care spending which comes from
government sources.

Data File: **NATIONS**
Task: **Mapping**
➤ *Variable 1:* **42) GOVT-HLT**
➤ *View:* **List: Rank**

RANK

U.S. ranking on government spending on health care   _____

Describe government spending on health care in the United States at the federal and state levels and
how it compares to that in other industrial countries.

8. Now let's return to public attitudes toward the government. First let's see if Democrats and
    Republicans differ in their opinion of the government.

➤ *Data File:* **NES**
➤ *Task:* **Cross-tabulation**
➤ *Row Variable:* **22) TRUST GOV**
➤ *Column Variable:* **43) POL.PARTY**
➤ *View:* **Table**
➤ *Display:* **Column %**

Copy the first line of the percentaged table.

	DEMOCRAT	INDEPENDENT	REPUBLICAN
Percentage who trust the government always or most of the time	_____%	_____%	_____%

What is the value of V for this table?   V = _____

Is V statistically significant?   Yes   No

➤ *Data File:* **GSS**
➤ *Task:* **Cross-tabulation**
➤ *Row Variable:* **31) FED.GOV'T**
➤ *Column Variable:* **62) POL.PARTY**
➤ *View:* **Table**
➤ *Display:* **Column %**

Copy the *first* line of the percentaged table.

	DEMOCRAT	INDEPENDENT	REPUBLICAN
Percentage who have some confidence	_____%	_____%	_____%

What is the value of V for this table?   V = _____

Is V statistically significant?   Yes   No

Circle the letter of the statement that provides the best summary of these two tables.

   a.   Democrats have more confidence in the federal government and are more likely to think that the government can be trusted.

   b.   Democrats have more confidence in the federal government; party has no effect on trust in the government.

   c.   Democrats have less confidence in the federal government and are more likely to think that the government can be trusted.

   d.   Democrats have less confidence in the federal government; party has no effect on trust in the government.

   e.   Democrats and Republicans are pretty much the same in their views of the federal government.

9.   Finally, let's see if there is a "gender gap" in evaluations of the government.

> *Data File:*   **NES**
> *Task:*   **Cross-tabulation**
> *Row Variable:*   **22) TRUST GOV**
> *Column Variable:*   **41) SEX**
> *View:*   **Table**
> *Display:*   **Column %**

Copy the *first* line of the percentaged table.

	MEN	WOMEN
Percentage who trust the government always or most of the time	_____%	_____%

What is the value of V for this table?   V = _____

Is V statistically significant?   Yes   No

> *Data File:*   **GSS**
> *Task:*   **Cross-tabulation**
> *Row Variable:*   **31) FED.GOV'T**
> *Column Variable:*   **61) SEX**
> *View:*   **Table**
> *Display:*   **Column %**

Copy the *first* line of the percentaged table.

	MEN	WOMEN
Percentage who have some confidence	_____%	_____%

What is the value of V for this table?   V = _____

Is V statistically significant?   Yes   No

Is there a gender gap in either confidence in or trust of the federal government?

EXERCISE **15**

THE COURTS

The judicial Power of the United States shall be vested in one supreme Court, and in such inferior Courts as the Congress may from time to time ordain and establish. The Judges, both of the supreme and inferior Courts, shall hold their Offices during good Behaviour, and shall, at stated Times, receive for their Services, a Compensation, which shall not be diminished during their Continuance in Office.

ARTICLE III, UNITED STATES
CONSTITUTION

Tasks: Mapping, Univariate, Cross-Tabulation, Historical Trends, Auto-Analyzer
Data Files: STATES, GSS, NES, HISTORY

The Supreme Court consists of nine justices, one of whom serves as chief justice. Justices are nominated by the president, and their appointment is confirmed (or rejected) by the Senate. Because all federal judges are appointed for life, the average term on the Court is quite long. Since the first justices were appointed in 1789, only 106 men and 2 women have served on the Court (Sandra Day O'Connor was appointed to the Court in 1981 by President Ronald Reagan, and Ruth Bader Ginsburg was appointed in 1993 by President Bill Clinton) and William Rehnquist is only the 15th chief justice.[1] Lifetime appointments also result in a relatively older Court—the average age was nearly 66 in 2000.

➤ *Data File:* **STATES**
➤ *Task:* **Mapping**
➤ *Variable 1:* **92) # S. COURT**
➤ *View:* **List: Rank**

RANK	CASE NAME	VALUE
1	New York	14
2	Ohio	9
2	Massachusetts	9
4	Virginia	8
5	Tennessee	6
5	Pennsylvania	6
7	Kentucky	5
8	Georgia	4
8	Maryland	4
8	California	4

[1] In 1975, John Rutledge served for four months while Congress recessed. The Senate rejected his nomination when Congress reconvened. Thus, some scholars say Rehnquist is the 16th chief justice.

Here we see the number of justices from each state. Understandably, the oldest states have more justices since they have had much greater opportunity. Nevertheless, the South has been somewhat overrepresented on the Court, five of the top twelve states being southern or border states. A total of 19 states never have had a justice.

The Constitution says nothing about the courts having the power to overrule Congress and to reject laws as unconstitutional. Rather, those who wrote the Constitution assumed that the courts would confine themselves to applying existing law to specific cases, and they never anticipated judges asserting new "laws" or discarding old ones. Thus, in *The Federalist* papers, Alexander Hamilton characterized the courts as the "least dangerous" and "the weakest" branch of government. However, in deciding a case in 1803, Chief Justice of the Supreme Court John Marshall asserted the right of the courts "to say what the law is." He further claimed that "a law repugnant to the Constitution is void." This position went unchallenged in Congress at that time and soon became the accepted view of Court power. This has resulted in frequent and often bitter conflicts between the Supreme Court, Congress, and the President. For example, President Franklin D. Roosevelt became so frustrated with rulings prohibiting many of his New Deal programs that in 1937 he proposed to "pack" the Court with new appointees. He asked Congress for legislation that would allow him to name an additional justice for every current member of the Court over age 70 (up to a total Court membership of 15), unless that judge retired, thus permitting appointment of a replacement. Since there were then six justices over 70, Roosevelt would have been able to appoint six new justices, giving his New Deal control of the Court. The bill did not pass and became irrelevant when a current justice switched to Roosevelt's side on issues.

Roosevelt was hardly alone in his antagonism toward the Supreme Court. Through the years the Supreme Court often has stirred up controversy by making decisions that many feel usurped the powers of Congress.

➤ *Data File:* **GSS**
➤ *Task:* **Univariate**
➤ *Primary Variable:* **7) SCH.PRAYER**
➤ *View:* **Pie**

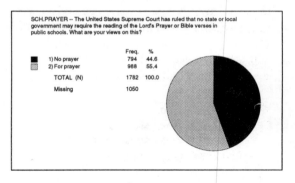

Although it has been more than 35 years since the Supreme Court prohibited prayer in the public schools (1962), this decision still has not gained general public acceptance. A large majority (55.4 percent) favor prayer in public schools. This is true even though the wording of the survey question maximizes support for the Court position since it does not deal with *allowing* prayer or Bible reading, but rather with laws *requiring* prayer or Bible reading.

Among the most controversial rulings are those interpreted by many as favoring the rights of criminals over those of victims of crimes. These concerns are not limited to the Supreme Court but are directed against the court system in general.

Data File: **GSS**
Task: **Univariate**
➤ Primary Variable: **30) COURTS?**
➤ View: **Pie**

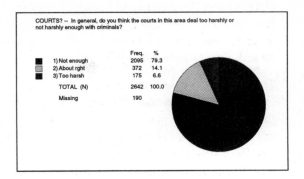

Americans overwhelmingly accuse the courts of not being sufficiently harsh in their treatment of criminals.

Data File: **GSS**
Task: **Univariate**
➤ Primary Variable: **35) SUP.COURT?**
➤ View: **Pie**

Given these results, it is not surprising that Americans are somewhat ambivalent about the Supreme Court. While about one in three expresses a great deal of confidence in the Court, more than half (52.5 percent) say they have "only some" confidence and 14.8 percent say they have "hardly any" confidence in the Court.

But, whatever they feel about the Court, what do Americans actually *know* about it? For example, how many even know the name of the chief justice?

➤ Data File: **NES**
➤ Task: **Univariate**
➤ Primary Variable: **16) CHIEF J.ID**
➤ View: **Pie**

When asked to name the job or political office held by William Rehnquist, only about one in ten could correctly identify him as the chief justice of the Supreme Court, thus revealing him to be the least-known major public official.

Data File: **NES**
➤ Task: **Cross-tabulation**
➤ Row Variable: **16) CHIEF J.ID**
➤ Column Variable: **14) NEWS TYPE**
➤ View: **Table**
➤ Display: **Column %**

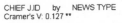

CHIEF J.ID by NEWS TYPE
Cramer's V: 0.127 **

		NEWS TYPE					
		TV&Paper	Paper	TV	Neither	Missing	TOTAL
CHIEF J.ID	Yes	34	37	19	46	0	136
		15.0%	17.0%	8.4%	7.6%		10.7%
	No	192	181	208	556	2	1137
		85.0%	83.0%	91.6%	92.4%		89.3%
	Missing	1	1	0	4	0	6
	TOTAL	226	218	227	602	2	1273
		100.0%	100.0%	100.0%	100.0%		

How do we learn the names of public officials? Obviously it's from the news media. Here we see a clear example of the differential impact of TV and newspapers in informing citizens. People who read newspapers every day, but do not watch TV news that often, are twice as likely to have correctly identified William Rehnquist than are those who rely only on TV for their daily news. And those who rely on both TV and newspapers are as likely to know Rehnquist as those who rely entirely on printed news.

A very plausible reason for the failure of TV to inform the public on many matters is that it is well known that TV scrimps on coverage of events for which it has no video and gives extra coverage, even to rather unimportant events, if it has good video. There is no video of the Supreme Court, so TV cannot let us see Rehnquist or other Court members in their official roles. Instead, important Supreme Court decisions usually are reported on TV by a reporter standing on the steps of the Court building and summarizing what the Court has done. Further, TV reports always are much shorter than the coverage given the same stories in newspapers—news stories usually contain many times more words than do the equivalent TV stories. As a result, the names of judges are mentioned far less often on TV than the names of other important officials.

The U.S. Supreme Court has many powers. It interprets laws and, occasionally, declares laws unconstitutional. But before the Supreme Court can issue a ruling on a case, it must first decide to hear that case. The Supreme Court selects to hear only a few cases from the thousands of cases appealed to it each year. Foremost the Supreme Court justices have time to hear only a select number of cases, as each case involves a number of stages from oral arguments, to preliminary discussion of decisions, to a final written opinion. By selecting among cases, the Court also demonstrates its power to decide what are the most important legal questions facing the nation. Let's examine both the number of cases appealed to the Supreme Court and the number of cases that conclude with a written opinion.

➤ Data File: **HISTORY**
➤ Task: **Historical Trends**
➤ Variables: **61) #CASE,S.CT**
          67) #S.C.DEC

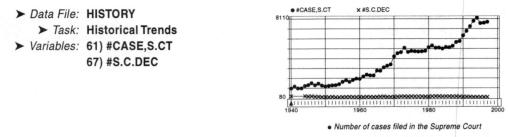

● Number of cases filed in the Supreme Court

✖ Number of Supreme Court cases decided by signed opinions

As you can see, the number of cases appealed to the Supreme Court has risen dramatically over the years, from slightly less than 1,000 in the 1940s to between 7,000 and 8,000 in the past decade. Yet, the

Part IV: Institutions

number of cases on which the Supreme Court issues a written opinion has varied only from 84 to 199. The Supreme Court simply refuses to hear more than 95 percent of the cases appealed to it. Since 1993, the Supreme Court has issued fewer than 100 written opinions each year, exercising even more control over its docket.

Your turn.

WORKSHEET

NAME:

COURSE:

DATE:

EXERCISE 15

REVIEW QUESTIONS

Based on the first part of this exercise, answer True or False to the following items:

There are 12 justices on the Supreme Court.	T	F
Bill Clinton was the first president to appoint a woman to the Court.	T	F
President Ronald Reagan became so angry about Supreme Court decisions that he asked Congress to let him "pack" the Court.	T	F
Federal judges are appointed for life.	T	F
Most Americans oppose prayer in public schools.	T	F
The Supreme Court issues a written opinion on 95 percent of the cases appealed to it.	T	F

EXPLORIT QUESTIONS

1. Questions about confidence in various institutions have been asked in the GSS since 1972. Let's see how confidence in the Supreme Court compares with confidence in Congress and in the government in general. Let's also include confidence in medicine, an institution outside of government, for a different perspective.

> *Data File:* **HISTORY**
> *Task:* **Historical Trends**
> *Variables:* **38) CONF CONG**
> **39) CONF COURT**
> **40) CONF GOV**
> **41) CONF MED**

Note that these are survey data so that the values are only estimates of the population values—changes or differences of less than 10 percent are probably not important.

Answer True or False to each of the following items:

People have more confidence in the medical profession than they do in the Supreme Court or Congress.	T	F

People have more confidence in Congress than they do in the Supreme Court.   T   F

Relative confidence in these institutions (medicine, Congress, the Supreme Court) fluctuates a great deal over time, so sometimes people have most confidence in medicine, sometimes Congress, and sometimes the Supreme Court.   T   F

2. Using the AUTO-ANALYZER task, let's see what demographic characteristics affect confidence in the Supreme Court.

> ➤ *Data File:* **GSS**
> ➤ *Task:* **Auto-Analyzer**
> ➤ *Variable:* **35) SUP.COURT?**

For each demographic variable listed below, indicate whether there is any significant effect. If so, indicate which category is most likely and which is least likely to have a great deal of confidence in the Supreme Court.

	IS THE EFFECT SIGNIFICANT?		CATEGORY MOST LIKELY TO HAVE A GREAT DEAL OF CONFIDENCE	CATEGORY LEAST LIKELY TO HAVE A GREAT DEAL OF CONFIDENCE
View: **Race**	Yes	No	_____	_____
View: **Religion**	Yes	No	_____	_____
View: **Education**	Yes	No	_____	_____

What are the characteristics of those most likely to have a great deal of confidence in the Court?

What are the characteristics of those least likely to have a great deal of confidence in the Court?

3. The Supreme Court has ruled on many controversial issues, and the ruling of the Court is not always popular. Perhaps an individual's attitude on these issues affects his or her confidence in the Court.

> Data File: **GSS**
> ➤ Task: **Cross-tabulation**
> ➤ Row Variable: **35) SUP.COURT?**
> ➤ Column Variable: **7) SCH.PRAYER**
> ➤ View: **Table**
> ➤ Display: **Column %**

Copy the *third* row of the percentaged table.

	NO PRAYER	FOR PRAYER
HARDLY ANY	_____%	_____%

What is the value of V for this table?   V = _____

Is V statistically significant?   Yes   No

One's attitude toward school prayer has an effect on one's confidence in the Supreme Court.   T   F

> Data File: **GSS**
> Task: **Cross-tabulation**
> Row Variable: **35) SUP.COURT?**
> ➤ Column Variable: **42) ABORT ANY**
> ➤ View: **Table**
> ➤ Display: **Column %**

Copy the *third* row of the percentaged table.

	APPROVE	DISAPPROVE
HARDLY ANY	_____%	_____%

What is the value of V for this table?   V = _____

Is V statistically significant?   Yes   No

One's attitude toward abortion has an effect on one's confidence in the Supreme Court.   T   F

Data File: **GSS**
Task: **Cross-tabulation**
Row Variable: **35) SUP.COURT?**
➤ Column Variable: **28) EXECUTE?**
➤ View: **Table**
➤ Display: **Column %**

Copy the *third* row of the percentaged table.

	FAVOR	**OPPOSE**
HARDLY ANY	_____%	_____%

What is the value of V for this table?   V = _____

Is V statistically significant?   Yes   No

One's attitude toward the death penalty has an effect on one's confidence in
the Supreme Court.   T   F

Taken together, these results suggest that confidence in the Supreme Court
is generally based on more than one issue.   T   F

4. In the GSS, respondents were asked who they would trust to make medical decisions for them if they
    were unable to do so.

Data File: **GSS**
➤ Task: **Univariate**
➤ Primary Variable: **52) TRUSTCRT**
➤ View: **Pie**

What percentage have a lot of trust in the courts to make this decision?   _____%

Data File: **GSS**
➤ Task: **Cross-tabulation**
➤ Row Variable: **52) TRUSTCRT**
➤ Column Variable: **35) SUP.COURT?**
➤ View: **Table**
➤ Display: **Column %**

Copy the *third* row of the percentaged table.

	GREAT DEAL	**ONLY SOME**	**HARDLY ANY**
LITTLE/NONE	_____%	_____%	_____%

What is the value of V for this table?   V = _____

Is V statistically significant?   Yes   No

Those who have a great deal of trust in the Supreme Court are more likely to
trust the courts to make medical decisions.   T   F

Everyone places a great deal of trust in the courts to make medical decisions.   T   F

5.   In the opening section of this exercise, we saw how the number of cases appealed to the Supreme Court has risen dramatically over the years. The Supreme Court, however, has control over its docket and can select to hear only a small fraction of these cases. The lowest level of the federal court system, the federal district court, does not have such discretionary control over the cases it hears. District courts are the starting point for criminal cases involving the violation of federal laws, though most criminal cases are heard in state courts. Federal district courts also hear civil cases, where one private party (e.g., an individual or a business) sues another private party for damages. Civil cases are heard in federal court if they involve parties from different states and seek damages over $75,000. Let's examine the number of criminal and civil cases heard in federal district court in the past 60 years.

> ➤ *Data File:* **HISTORY**
> ➤ *Task:* **Historical Trends**
> ➤ *Variables:* **64) #CIV COM**
>   **65) #CRIM COM**

The workload (combined total of criminal and civil cases) before the federal
district court has risen dramatically over the past 60 years.   T   F

The change in the workload of the federal district court is due mainly to a large
change in the number of criminal cases.   T   F

APPENDIX: VARIABLE NAMES AND SOURCES

◆ DATA FILE: COLONIAL ◆

1) CASE ID
2) POP 1790
3) %BRITISH
4) % PROT.
5) # SLAVES
6) %SLAVES 90
7) #FREE AFR.

8) % FREE
9) # AFRI.-AM
10) %BLACK 90
11) CHURCHED76
12) WHITE CH76
13) %R CATH 76
14) %ENGLISH90

15) %SCOTCH 90
16) %P.IRISH 90
17) %C.IRISH90
18) %GERMAN90
19) %DUTCH 90
20) %FRENCH 90
21) %SWEDISH90

◆ DATA FILE: COUNTY ◆

1) NAME
2) POPULATION
3) %WHITE
4) %BLACK
5) %HISPANIC
6) %HISPANIC2
7) %MEXICAN
8) %MEXICAN2
9) %AMER.IND
10) %AMER.IND2
11) %ASIAN

12) %ASIAN2
13) %NORWEG
14) %IRISH
15) %GERMAN
16) %FOREIGN
17) %FOREIGN2
18) %NON-ENGL
19) %POOR
20) MED.FAM$
21) FARM %
22) MANUFACT%

23) %NO MOVE
24) %<5 90
25) %>64 90
26) DEATH 88
27) CHLD MRT88
28) %EMERG.90
29) CHLD POR89
30) H.S.GRAD90
31) COL.DEGR90

◆ DATA FILE: GSS ◆

1) OVER 50
2) OVER 30
3) WH/AFR.AM
4) # CHILDREN
5) LIB./CONS.
6) ATTEND
7) SCH.PRAYER
8) COLLEGE/NT
9) EVER UNEMP
10) UNIONIZED?
11) HAPPY?
12) PAR. BORN?
13) OWN GUN?
14) HUNT?
15) NEWSPAPER?
16) WATCH TV
17) WHO IN 92?
18) VOTE 92?

19) WHO IN 96?
20) VOTE 96?
21) MEN BETTER
22) WOMAN PRES
23) ATHEIST SP
24) COMMUN.SP
25) RACIST SP
26) FR.SPEECH
27) TAXES?
28) EXECUTE?
29) GUN LAW?
30) COURTS?
31) FED.GOV'T
32) LABOR?
33) PRESS?
34) SCIENCE?
35) SUP.COURT?
36) CONGRESS?

37) MILITARY?
38) BIG BIZ?
39) EDUCATION?
40) ABORT.WANT
41) ABORT.HLTH
42) ABORT ANY
43) PORN.LAW?
44) SUIC.WISH
45) FOR. AID $
46) DEFENSE $
47) WAR IN 10?
48) WELFARE $
49) POOR $
50) TRUSTFAM
51) TRUSTDOC
52) TRUSTCRT
53) INC. DIF?
54) RELPREF ST

◆ DATA FILE: GSS (cont'd) ◆

55) URBAN?
56) SOC.SEC$
57) BIG CITY$
58) BLACK $
59) MASS TRAN$
60) DEM/REP
61) SEX
62) POL.PARTY
63) MARITAL
64) RELIGION
65) REGION
66) AGE
67) EDUCATION
68) INCOME
69) RACE
70) DAD EDUC.

71) MOM EDUC.
72) IF:WHO 92?
73) IF:WHO 96?
74) WOMEN HOME
75) WOMEN WORK
76) HOMO.SEX
77) EUTHANASIA
78) MUCH GOVNT
79) GOV.MED.
80) GOV. BLACK
81) HMO1
82) HMO4
83) SOCSECRT
84) SOCSECFX
85) SOCSECNU
86) JOBS ALL

87) CHEAT1
88) CHEAT2
89) RELIGIOUS2
90) RELIGIOUS4
91) R.FUND/LIB
92) INTERMAR.?
93) BELIEV.GOD
94) PRAY
95) BIBLE1
96) READ BIBLE
97) REBORN
98) LESSPAIN
99) RELPERSN
100) SEX OF SEX

◆ DATA FILE: HOUSE106 ◆

1) NAME
2) SEX
3) RACE/ETHNI
4) AGE
5) RELIGION
6) EDUCATION
7) MARITAL
8) LAWYER?
9) PARTY
10) SOUTH DEM
11) INCUMBENT
12) # TERMS
13) TERM LIMIT
14) STATE
15) REGION
16) DISTRICT#
17) % OF VOTE
18) $REP $OPPO
19) OPPONENT$
20) %PAC CONTR
21) CAMPAIGN $
22) $ PER VOTE
23) DIS HOUSE$
24) DIS FAMINC
25) DIST HISP%
26) DIS AFRAM%

27) ACLU RATE
28) ADA RATE
29) ACU RATE
30) TROOPS1
31) TROOPS2
32) NOABORTDRG
33) JUVOFFCONS
34) IMPCH-MANG
35) PEACECORPS
36) STL IMPORT
37) REC MISDEF
38) MISL DEFEN
39) CENSUS REV
40) MEDIA JUVN
41) REL ESTAB
42) TEN COMMAN
43) GUN SAFETY
44) FLAG DESCR
45) STATEABORT
46) CONSERVTN$
47) LOWER NEA$
48) NATFORST $
49) RELIB CLMS
50) RELIG LIB
51) NOCHNABOR
52) LIMIT ADPT

53) LEGL SERV$
54) HOPA$
55) CAMP FINAN
56) UNBORN
57) INTERIOR
58) MANGD CARE
59) ANML CRUEL
60) CHNGE SCHL
61) PAIN CARE
62) TAIWAN
63) BUSNS SUIT
64) BUSNS LIAB
65) MINWAGE
66) MINWAGE2
67) SENIORWORK
68) PARTBIRTH
69) TAXLIMIT
70) INTERNET
71) CONSERVE
72) CHINA
73) ESTATE TAX
74) PRESCRIPT
75) MARRY TAX
76) SSINCTAX

◆ DATA FILE: USPRES ◆

1) namyear
2) NAME
3) YEAR
4) ELECTVOTE
5) POPVOTE
6) PARTY
7) EARLY
8) PRESNUMBER
9) ELECT AGE
10) HEIGHT
11) EDUCATION
12) LAWYER

13) MILITARY
14) MIL FAME
15) RELIGION
16) HOW RELIG
17) YRS IN OFF
18) VETOES
19) ASSASSIN
20) ETHNICITY
21) GOV?
22) SEN?
23) VEEP?
24) RATING

25) SUP CT
26) TOT JUDGES
27) CENTURY
28) PTY-CONG
29) OVERRIDE
30) UNELECT
31) # VPRES
32) SEC ELEC C
33) SEC POP VT
34) MINOR
35) ERA

◆ DATA FILE: NATIONS ◆

1) COUNTRY
2) POP98
3) P.INTEREST
4) TALK POL.
5) PERSUASION
6) PETITION?
7) INTEREST G
8) SIT-INS
9) REVOLUTION
10) LEFT/RIGHT
11) ANTI-RACE
12) ANTI-FORGN
13) ANTI-JEW
14) ANTI-GAY
15) %FEM LEGIS

16) %FEM HEADS
17) WOMEN WANT
18) DEMOCRACY
19) CIVIL LIBS
20) VERY HAPPY
21) NATL PRIDE
22) PRESS?
23) PARLIAMENT
24) UNIONS?
25) WORK PRIDE
26) CHEAT TAX
27) TAKE BRIBE
28) CARS/CAP
29) % URBAN
30) NEWSPAPERS

31) TELEVISION
32) LITERACY
33) ABRT.UNWED
34) A.UNWANT
35) GDP/CAP
36) # PARTIES
37) %BIG PARTY
38) % VOTED
39) FIGHT COPS
40) EDUC EXPTD
41) HEALTH
42) GOVT-HLT
43) MIL-GNP
44) MIL-PC

◆ DATA FILE: NES ◆

1) VOTE?
2) PRES IN 96
3) INTEREST?
4) IDEOLOGY
5) INFORMED?
6) TV NEWS?
7) READ PAPER
8) CALL RADIO
9) UNION?
10) PRTY TALK

11) TALK POL?
12) BUTTON
13) CANDID.$
14) NEWS TYPE
15) RUSSIAN ID
16) CHIEF J.ID
17) VEEP ID
18) TRUST NEWS
19) PARTY $
20) ANY TALK

21) TALK REG
22) TRUST GOV
23) GORE RATE
24) BUSH RATE
25) DOLE RATE
26) BRAD.RATE
27) GORE KNOW
28) BUSH KNOW
29) DOLE KNOW
30) BRAD. KNOW

◆ DATA FILE: NES (cont'd) ◆

31) DISC. POL?
32) AFFIRM.ACT
33) OFF LANG?
34) WOMEN EQL
35) EQUAL RGT
36) BLEND IN?
37) HISPANIC
38) DEM/REP
39) VOTED 98?
40) REGISTERED
41) SEX
42) RACE
43) POL.PARTY
44) MARITAL
45) RELIGION
46) REGION
47) AGE
48) EDUCATION
49) INCOME
50) WOM EQ DEM
51) WOM EQ REP
52) SCHL PRAY
53) RELIG POL
54) RELIG.POL2
55) IMP. RELIG
56) PRAYER

57) GODS WORD
58) ATTEND FRQ
59) ABORTION
60) ABORTION D
61) ABORTION R
62) LATE TERM
63) CLINTON
64) CARE HOUSE
65) KNOW HOUSE
66) CONGRESS
67) WHO HSE?
68) WHO SEN PR
69) WHO GUV PR
70) APPRV INC2
71) TERM LIMIT
72) FOLOW GOV
73) PARTY DIFF
74) CRIME PRTY
75) ECON. PRTY
76) POLLUT PRT
77) FORGN PRTY
78) SOC.SEC PT
79) FAMLY PRTY
80) SCALE DEMS
81) SCALE REPS
82) ECONOMY

83) PTY CONTRL
84) PARTIES
85) JOB GUAR
86) SPENDING
87) SPENDING D
88) SPENDING R
89) SCHL VOUCH
90) STRONG US
91) STAY HOME
92) IMMIGRATE
93) IMPORTS
94) ENV REGS
95) ENV REGS D
96) ENV REGS R
97) DEATH PEN
98) FAMILY VAL
99) MAKE DIFF
100) GOVT ATTN
101) ELECT ATTN
102) COMPLICATE
103) DON'T CARE
104) NO SAY
105) CROOKED?
106) GOVT WASTE
107) BIG INTERS
108) NO PARTIES

◆ DATA FILE: STATES ◆

1) STATE NAME
2) POPULATION
3) BIG REGION
4) URBAN USA
5) %URBAN'00
6) SUNBELT
7) THE WEST
8) THE SOUTH
9) SLAVE/FREE
10) UNION/CONF
11) STATES1860
12) MOBILE HOM
13) FAMILY $
14) HIGH $
15) %POOR
16) FED$ RATIO
17) %FED LAND

18) FED.EMPLOY
19) DEFENSE $
20) INCOME TAX
21) STATE DEBT
22) %FOREIGN
23) % WHITE
24) %AFRIC.AM
25) % ASIAN
26) %HISPANIC
27) %SPAN.SPK
28) POP GROW
29) NEW HOMES
30) MALE HOMES
31) N.R./NAT.
32) %FEMALE LG
33) % VOTED'92
34) %REGIST.92

35) STATES '92
36) CLINTON'92
37) %BUSH '92
38) %PEROT 92
39) STATES '88
40) %BUSH '88
41) STATES '84
42) %REAGAN 84
43) STATES '80
44) %REAGAN'80
45) %CARTER'80
46) %ANDERSON
47) STATES '76
48) %CARTER 76
49) STATES '72
50) %NIXON '72
51) STATES '68

52) % NIXON'68
53) %HUMPH.'68
54) %WALLACE68
55) STATES '64
56) %JOHNSON64
57) STATES '60
58) %KENNEDY60
59) STATES '56
60) IKE '56
61) STATES '52
62) %IKE '52
63) STATES'48
64) %TRUMAN
65) %DEWEY'48
66) %THURMD'48
67) %WALLACE48
68) STATES '44
69) % FDR '44
70) STATES '40
71) % FDR '40
72) STATES '36
73) FDR '36
74) STATES '32
75) FDR '32
76) STATES '28
77) %HOOVER'28
78) STATES '24
79) %COOL '24
80) %LAFOLL.24
81) STATES '20
82) %HARDING20
83) % LEFT '20
84) ELECTOR90
85) ELECTOR60
86) ELECTOR40
87) EC GAIN60
88) PRESIDENTS
89) UN/CONF SL
90) %SLAV ST
91) # HOUSE
92) # S. COURT
93) %CLINTON96
94) %DOLE 96
95) %PEROT96
96) STATES '96
97) %VOTED 96
98) %REGIST.96

99) DEBT$/CAP
100) POP GO
101) DIF.ST.
102) SPEEDING
103) WELFARE
104) TOUGH LOVE
105) $ HI ED.
106) %HI EDUC $
107) STA EX/CAP
108) EDUC$/CAP
109) HLTH$/CAP
110) WELF$/CAP
111) HGHWYS$/CA
112) CORR$/CAP
113) FED$/CAP
114) PROP.TAX
115) VIOL.CRIME
116) MURDER
117) POP 98
118) RAPE
119) ROBBERY
120) ASSAULT
121) BURGLARY
122) LARCENY
123) PROP CRIME
124) HEALTH INS
125) %COLLEGE
126) %HIGH SCH
127) HATECRIMES
128) POLICE
129) #SOC.SEC
130) SS BENEFIT
131) %SOCSEC
132) UNEMP $
133) AVG ENEMP$
134) UNEMP$/CAP
135) AVG PAY
136) PER CAP$
137) STATE TAX
138) EXPENDITUR
139) TANF FAM#
140) TANF FAM
141) ABORTRATE
142) $PER PUPIL
143) TOXIC
144) LOC$/CAP
145) LOCEX$/CAP

146) FEDFUNDS
147) FDAID-CHFM
148) FDAID-HOUS
149) MED AGE
150) UNEMPLOY
151) % UNION
152) CIG TAX
153) %FOODSTAMP
154) DEM LEGIS
155) REPUB LEGI
156) DEM-REPS
157) REPUB-REPS
158) DEM-SENS
159) REPUB-SENS
160) DEM CONG
161) REPUB CONG
162) PCOMP-CONG
163) PCOMP-LEG
164) MOTOR VTR
165) POP GROW2
166) DTH OPIN
167) DTH LAW
168) LIBERAL
169) MODERATE
170) CONSER
171) POP-DEM
172) POP-IND
173) POP-REP
174) PROCHOICE
175) PROLIFE
176) BS-VISITS
177) GR-VISITS
178) GORE
179) GWBUSH
180) NADER
181) BUCHANAN
182) THIRDPTY
183) MARGIN
184) MARGINP
185) STATES '00
186) GWB-ECVOTE
187) GORE-ECVOT
188) COMPETITIV
189) GORENADER
190) ELECTOR00
191) EC GAIN00
192) HOUSE03

◆ TREND FILE: HISTORY ◆

1) DATE
2) POPULATION
3) %<5
4) %65&OVER
5) % URBAN
6) %HS
7) %COLLEGE
8) %NO HS
9) LAWYER/CAP
10) DOCTOR/CAP
11) CPI(1967)
12) VOTER PART
13) % DEM
14) % REP
15) APPORTION
16) %DEM HOUSE
17) D.PRES %
18) M.D.PRES %
19) F.D.PRES %
20) W.D.PRES %
21) B.D.PRES %
22) %HH TELE
23) TV VIEW
24) READ PAPER

25) NEWS/100
26) TV/100HH
27) SOUTH.DEM
28) CIVLIB INX
29) %FEM PRES
30) %M F.PRES
31) %F F.PRES
32) % BLK PRES
33) GOV.CROOK?
34) TRUST GOV
35) WASTE TAX
36) CONF.TV
37) CONF.PRESS
38) CONF CONG
39) CONF COURT
40) CONF GOV
41) CONF MED
42) CONF MIL
43) ENVIR $
44) DEFENSE $
45) WELF $
46) HEALTH $
47) BLACK $
48) DRUG $

49) FED EMP RT
50) DEF EMP RT
51) LEG EMP RT
52) JUDG EMP R
53) NON-D EMP
54) DEF$/POP
55) HR$/POP
56) S.S.$/POP
57) I.S.$/POP
58) MED$/POP
59) HEAL$/POP
60) ED$/POP
61) #CASE,S.CT
62) #CASE COMM
63) #CRIM CASE
64) #CIV COM
65) #CRIM COM
66) RACE SEG
67) #S.C.DEC
68) HSE-OTH
69) SEN-OTH
70) %REP HOUSE
71) DEM$
72) REP$

Appendix: Variable Names and Sources

SOURCES

NES–National Election Study, 1998

The NES data file is based on selected variables from the 1998 American National Election Study provided by the National Election Studies, Institute for Social Research at the University of Michigan and the Inter-university Consortium for Political and Social Research. The principal investigators are Steven J. Rosenstone, Warren E. Miller, Donald R. Kinder, and the National Election Studies.

GSS–General Social Survey

The GSS data file is based on selected variables from the National Opinion Research Center (University of Chicago) General Social Surveys for 1998, distributed by The Roper Center and the Inter-university Consortium for Political and Social Research. The principal investigators are James A. Davis and Tom W. Smith.

STATES–The Fifty States of the U.S.

The data in the STATES file are from a variety of sources. The variable description for each variable uses the following abbreviations to indicate the source.

> ABC: Blue Book, Audit Bureau of Circulation
> CENSUS: The summary volumes of the 1990 U.S. Census
> CHRON.: The Chronicle of Higher Education Almanac
> DES: Digest of Education Statistics, U.S. Dept. of Education
> FEC: Federal Election Commission
> HCSR: Health Care State Rankings, Morgan Quitno
> HIGHWAY: Highway Statistics, Federal Highway Administration, U.S. Dept. of Transportation
> KOSMIN: Kosmin, Barry A. 1991. Research Report: The National Survey of Religious
>   Identification. New York: CUNY Graduate Center.
> SMAD: State and Metropolitan Area Data Book, 1991, U.S. Dept. of Commerce
> SOS: Secretary of State or Election Board web pages
> S.P.R.: State Policy Reference
> S.R.: State Rankings, Morgan Quitno
> UCR: Uniform Crime Reports, U.S. Dept. of Justice

NATIONS–Nations of the World

The data in the NATIONS file are from a variety of sources. The variable description for each variable uses the following abbreviations to indicate the source.

> ABC: Blue Book, Audit Bureau of Circulation
> DES: Digest of Education Statistics, U.S. Dept. of Education
> ES: Electoral Studies
> FITW: Freedom in the World, 1995, Freedom House
> HDR: Human Development Reports, United Nations Development Program
> PRB: World Population Data Sheet, 1994, Population Research Council
> SA: Statistical Abstract of the United States
> TWF: The World Fact Book, 1994–1995, Central Intelligence Agency
> WABF: The World Almanac and Book of Facts, 1995

WVS: World Values Survey, Institute for Social Research, Inter-University Consortium for Political and Social Research

USPRES—Presidents of the United States

The data in the USPRES file are from a variety of readily available sources, such as a world almanac or an encyclopedia, the Census, or other government publications. The variable description for each variable uses the following abbreviations to indicate the source.

NARA: National Archives and Records Administration "Electoral College Box Scores" on web page.

CWP: Congressional Web Pages, Gary L. Galemore, "Presidential Vetoes, 1789–1996: A Summary Overview," CRS Report for Congress, htttp://www.house.gov/rules/97–163.htm. Udpated will Bill Summary & Status, 105th Congree, Vetoed Bills, House Webpages. "Political Divisions of the House of Representatives, 1789–present," http://clerkweb.house.gov/histrecs/househist/lists/divisionh.htm. "Senate Statistics: Majority and Minority Parties," http://www.senate.gov/learning/stat_13.htm.

FWP: Federal Judiciary Web Pages, "Judgeship Appointments by Presidents," http://www.uscourts.gov/history/table1.pdf.

COLONIAL—The Thirteen Colonies plus Georgia and Maine

The data in the COLONIAL file are from a variety of readily available sources, such as a world almanac or encyclopedia, the U.S. Census, or other government publications.

HOUSE106

The data in the HOUSE106 file are from a variety of readily available sources, such as a world almanac or encyclopedia, the U.S. Census, the Thomas web site (http://thomas.loc.gov), or other government publications.